Wayne .

Wayne Larsen is a landscape painter, newspaper editor, and columnist whose work has appeared in a wide variety of print and online publications. He grew up in Montreal's east end and in Val David, Quebec, where he spent a lot of time fishing and climbing mountains.

He is currently a full-time professor in the Journalism Department at Concordia University. His freelance career has included work as a news and feature writer for the *Montreal Gazette*, as well as a copy editor at *Reader's Digest Canada*. From 2000 to 2010 he was editor-in-chief of the *Westmount Examiner*, during which period the paper won several awards for excellence.

As an artist, he has painted the landscapes of several different regions of Canada. He has always been especially interested in Tom Thomson and the Group of Seven, and, as a result, he is often invited to lecture on twentieth-century Canadian art and media issues.

Tom Thomson: Artist of the North is Wayne's fourth book. He has previously written biographies of A.Y. Jackson and James Wilson Morrice. His full-length biography *A.Y. Jackson: The Life of a Landscape Painter* reached the number-two position on the *Globe and Mail* bestseller list (art books).

He currently lives in Montreal with his wife, art historian Darlene Cousins, and their children, Nikolas and Bryn-Vienna.

In the same collection

Ven Begamudré, *Isaac Brock: Larger Than Life*
Lynne Bowen, *Robert Dunsmuir: Laird of the Mines*
Kate Braid, *Emily Carr: Rebel Artist*
Kathryn Bridge, *Phyllis Munday: Mountaineer*
Edward Butts, *Henry Hudson: New World Voyager*
William Chalmers, *George Mercer Dawson: Geologist, Scientist, Explorer*
Anne Cimon, *Susanna Moodie: Pioneer Author*
Deborah Cowley, *Lucille Teasdale: Doctor of Courage*
Gary Evans, *John Grierson: Trailblazer of Documentary Film*
Julie H. Ferguson, *James Douglas: Father of British Columbia*
Judith Fitzgerald, *Marshall McLuhan: Wise Guy*
lian goodall, *William Lyon Mackenzie King: Dreams and Shadows*
Tom Henighan, *Vilhjalmur Stefansson: Arctic Adventurer*
Stephen Eaton Hume, *Frederick Banting: Hero, Healer, Artist*
Naïm Kattan, *A.M. Klein: Poet and Prophet*
Betty Keller, *Pauline Johnson: First Aboriginal Voice of Canada*
Heather Kirk, *Mazo de la Roche: Rich and Famous Writer*
Valerie Knowles, *William C. Van Horne: Railway Titan*
Vladimir Konieczny, *Glenn Gould: A Musical Force*
Michelle Labrèche-Larouche, *Emma Albani: International Star*
D.H. Lahey, *George Simpson: Blaze of Glory*
Wayne Larsen, *A.Y. Jackson: A Love for the Land*
Wayne Larsen, *James Wilson Morrice: Painter of Light and Shadow*
Francine Legaré, *Samuel de Champlain: Father of New France*
Margaret Macpherson, *Nellie McClung: Voice for the Voiceless*
Nicholas Maes, *Robertson Davies: Magician of Words*
Dave Margoshes, *Tommy Douglas: Building the New Society*
Marguerite Paulin, *René Lévesque: Charismatic Leader*
Raymond Plante, *Jacques Plante: Behind the Mask*
Jim Poling Sr., *Tecumseh: Shooting Star, Crouching Panther*
T.F. Rigelhof, *George Grant: Redefining Canada*
Tom Shardlow, *David Thompson: A Trail by Stars*
Arthur Slade, *John Diefenbaker: An Appointment with Destiny*
Roderick Stewart, *Wilfrid Laurier: A Pledge for Canada*
Sharon Stewart, *Louis Riel: Firebrand*
André Vanasse, *Gabrielle Roy: A Passion for Writing*
John Wilson, *John Franklin: Traveller on Undiscovered Seas*
John Wilson, *Norman Bethune: A Life of Passionate Conviction*
Rachel Wyatt, *Agnes Macphail: Champion of the Underdog*

A QUEST BIOGRAPHY

TOM THOMSON

ARTIST OF THE NORTH

WAYNE LARSEN

DUNDURN PRESS
TORONTO

Project Editor: Michael Carroll
Editor: Jennifer McKnight
Design: Jennifer Scott
Printer: Webcom

Library and Archives Canada Cataloguing in Publication

Larsen, Wayne, 1961-
     Tom Thomson : artist of the North / by Wayne Larsen.

Includes bibliographical references and index.
Issued also in an electronic format.
ISBN 978-1-55488-772-9

1. Thomson, Tom, 1877-1917. 2. Group of Seven (Group of artists). 3. Painters--Canada--Biography. 4. Landscape painting, Canadian--20th century. I. Title.

ND249.T5L372 2010   759.11   C2010-902700-0

1   2   3   4   5   15   14   13   12   11

Conseil des Arts du Canada   Canada Council for the Arts   Canadä   ONTARIO ARTS COUNCIL CONSEIL DES ARTS DE L'ONTARIO

We acknowledge the support of the Canada Council for the Arts and the Ontario Arts Council for our publishing program. We also acknowledge the financial support of the Government of Canada through the Canada Book Fund and Livres Canada Books, and the Government of Ontario through the Ontario Book Publishers Tax Credit program, and the Ontario Media Development Corporation.

Care has been taken to trace the ownership of copyright material used in this book. The author and the publisher welcome any information enabling them to rectify any references or credits in subsequent editions.

J. Kirk Howard, President

www.dundurn.com

Dundurn Press
3 Church Street, Suite 500
Toronto, Ontario, Canada
M5E 1M2

Gazelle Book Services Limited
White Cross Mills
High Town, Lancaster, England
LA1 4XS

Dundurn Press
2250 Military Road
Tonawanda, NY
U.S.A. 14150

To Darlene, as always …

Contents

Acknowledgements

A biography of this nature is built largely upon facts unearthed by others, and to that end I would like to acknowledge my debt to the research and scholarship of Charles C. Hill, Joan Murray, Dennis Reid, and David Silcox, whose previous works on Tom Thomson and his contemporaries have helped to put his life into perspective.

I would also like to acknowledge Peter Downie for his constant interest in this project and his many helpful suggestions. Thank you, Komrade!

At Dundurn, many thanks to Jennifer McKnight for her diligent work on the manuscript — not to mention photography service above and beyond the call — and to Michael Carroll for his guidance and enthusiasm for this project from the very beginning. My thanks also go to Kirk Howard, Karen McMullin, and Marta Warner for their hard work and support.

Thanks to Karen Forbes Cutler for her photo of the Studio Building; to Bill Thornley for providing the idyllic winter writing space; and for their help in a variety of ways, thank you to Alan Aitken, Doreen Lindsay, Terry Rigelhof, and Marilynn Vanderstaay. I'd also like to thank Ron Tozer from The Friends of Algonquin Park for providing photos from the Algonquin Park Archives.

Thanks also to my children, Nik and Bryn, who always seem to be called upon to perform some task during the writing and research process and always come through.

And, as always, special thanks to my wife, art historian Darlene Cousins, without whose advice and support this book would not have been possible.

Introduction

This is the story of an Ontario farm boy who turned his life-long passion for the northern wilderness into a brief but brilliant career as a landscape artist.

Nearly a century has passed since Tom Thomson's mysterious death in Algonquin Park, but Canada's fascination with this shadowy figure refuses to abate. He has grown into an icon of our culture, arguably a close second to Emily Carr as Canada's best-known and most venerated artist. Some of the images he created are now as familiar to many Canadians as the logos of Tim Hortons, the CBC, and the National Hockey League. It is highly unlikely that anyone could spend a year in this country without once encountering the weathered old trees of Thomson's *The Jack Pine* or *The West Wind*, either in their original forms or as commercial parodies.

Thomson's short life has been briefly chronicled in several books, most of which were produced since the 1960s, when Canadians "rediscovered" Thomson along with his close friends, the Group of Seven, and began viewing their work with renewed interest. But many details of Thomson's life remain sketchy: he was not a prolific letter writer, and attempts to piece together a full-length biography were always doomed from the outset by a lack of concrete facts. This problem was compounded by hearsay and second-hand stories repeated by those too young to have known Thomson personally and the foggy, faltering memories of those who did. Only recently, thanks to some long-overdue detective work chronicled in Roy MacGregor's excellent book *Northern Light*, has a portion of the ninety-three-year-old mystery of Thomson's death been solved and the matter finally laid to rest — in this case quite literally.

But still, many other questions remain unanswered. From books and documentary films to a (believe it or not!) Tom Thomson Murder Mystery party game, the entire Thomson saga has mushroomed into a fascinating element of Canadian culture. Tom Thomson is as much a part of our national fabric as Sir John A. Macdonald and Samuel de Champlain. He was hailed as a hero by his friends and fellow artists — a sentiment gleefully perpetuated through the generations by many art historians — yet Thomson himself was the unlikeliest of heroes. He was a quiet, simple man, often shy and awkward with women, who would eventually choose to spend as much time as possible paddling his canoe through his beloved Algonquin Park. It was there, in this paradise of woods and water, that he could finally devote nearly all of his energy to his two greatest passions — painting and fishing.

As a result, this is a book about fishing almost as much as it is about art, for in Thomson's case the two were so closely intertwined. The only constant in his life was fishing; from idyllic boyhood afternoons spent on riverbanks near Owen Sound to what is widely believed to be the very moment he died, his fishing rod was always with him.

Painting and fishing both require patience and skill, and success rarely comes without a struggle. The artist can lose a painting on the panel or canvas just as easily as an angler can lose a fish off the hook. Whenever an interesting subject caught Thomson's eye, be it a deep blue tangle of shadows on a snow-covered embankment or a cluster of blazing yellow tamaracks by the edge of a lake, he opened his sketch box and set to work painting with the same optimism as a trout fisherman casting his line into a deep, dark pool at the side of a rushing river, hoping to land that elusive big one.

And sometimes Thomson landed a very big one indeed. Anyone doubting this need only look closely at the intricate screen of dead spruce trees in the foreground of *Northern River*, the force of a spring gale on a wilderness lake in *The West Wind*, and the solemn dignity of a weather-beaten *Jack Pine* standing alone and defiant against the northern elements.

The myths and legends surrounding Tom Thomson's life and death are likely to continue for many years to come. But through all the controversy we can always be sure of one thing — during those last few years of his life, when he could fish and paint to his heart's content, he rarely returned to camp empty-handed.

The jealous trout, that low did lie
Rose at a well-dissembled fly
There stood my Friend, with patient skill,
Attending of his trembling quill.

— Izaak Walton, *The Compleat Angler*

1

An Excavation at Canoe Lake

A chilly October wind blew across the southwestern corner of Algonquin Park, shaking the fir trees and sending droplets of rain down onto the four men who made their way through the wet woods. Most of the maples and birches had lost their leaves, offering no protection from the steady drizzle.

Dressed in loose-fitting work clothes — wide-brimmed hats, old flannel plaid shirts, and long trench coats to protect them from the rain and dripping branches — the men carried knapsacks and each had a shovel or axe slung over his shoulder. They passed single-file along a narrow, muddy path running parallel to the shoreline.

A few metres away, silvery-white Canoe Lake sat cold and uninviting in the rain.

Soon the men were heading inland, their backs to the lake, and the woods got thicker.

"Are you sure it's around here?" one of them asked.

"Not much farther," another replied.

"We're looking for a big old birch tree."

"Plenty to choose from around here!"

"This one stands out from all the others. I'll know it when I see it."

The men pressed on through the underbrush. Here and there were traces of an old path, which made the going a bit easier for a few minutes, but the bush always closed back in. It was obvious that no one had been up there in a long time.

After trudging along for half an hour, they finally emerged from the thick woods and climbed to the top of a low bluff. They found themselves in a clearing just beyond the northwest shore of the lake.

"This is it," said Leonard "Gibby" Gibson, a Canoe Lake native who knew the area well and was acting as unofficial guide. "This is definitely it."

Bill Little and Frank Braught dropped their shovels and knapsacks, while Jack Eastaugh lit his pipe and gazed around at the scene. Gibby was right. The birch tree was unmistakable — it was huge and ancient, with massive branches extending out at odd horizontal angles. Beneath it, a crude, weathered old wooden picket fence poked up from the tangled brush. Away in the background, the lake was barely visible as a ribbon of white in the distance.

"Welcome to the old Canoe Lake Cemetery, gentlemen," said Gibby.

After some discussion as to where they should start, the men carefully examined the surrounding terrain and finally decided on a promising spot near the birch tree. They set to work ripping out a few saplings and clearing away the underbrush with

Courtesy Algonquin Park Museum Archives #6739 (Tom Little).

Hoping to solve the mystery of Tom Thomson's final resting place, four friends decide to find his grave. From left: Leonard Gibson, William Little, Frank Braught, and Jack Eastaugh at the Canoe Lake cemetery in 1956.

their axes, and soon the first shovel blades were slicing into the sandy earth.

The men dug in silence for half an hour. The only sounds came from their shovels and the grunt of exertion, broken occasionally by a cacophony of honking overhead as the last few lines of Canada geese headed south for the winter.

"I just thought of something," said Little. "It sure is a good thing it's a lousy day and there's not likely to be anyone hiking in these woods right now. If they came upon four guys digging up a remote gravesite, they might get the wrong idea."

The others chuckled as they worked, for they knew that what they were doing would certainly appear sinister at first. In fact, the men were searching for the answer to a mystery that had been haunting the residents of Canoe Lake — and countless other Canadians — for longer than most people could remember.

Nearly forty years earlier, an up-and-coming artist from Toronto had drowned in Canoe Lake. He was said to have been a strong swimmer and an expert at handling a canoe, so the circumstances surrounding his death had always been a mystery to the inhabitants of Canoe Lake.

Normally, the story of a local drowning would have grown stale over the years and perhaps been forgotten, but this case was special. The artist's reputation had grown quickly after his untimely death, and soon the name Tom Thomson was known across Canada as one of the nation's most innovative landscape painters. His images of the northern wilderness — most of which were sketched at or near Canoe Lake in Algonquin Park — were familiar to many Canadians. Reproductions of his two most famous paintings, *The West Wind* and *The Jack Pine*, were not only displayed on the walls of banks, libraries, and classrooms across the nation, but had also become symbols of the north country itself — a weather-beaten old tree overlooking a wilderness lake, standing alone and strong against the harsh elements.

As Thomson's fame grew, so did speculation over his mysterious drowning in Canoe Lake back in 1917. Various conspiracy theories made strong arguments for murder, while other viewpoints supported evidence of an accident. Theories were one thing, but with no physical evidence to support either side of the argument, Canadians would never know what had really happened to their most venerated landscape artist.

There was even speculation about Thomson's final resting place. He was originally buried in the tiny cemetery at Canoe Lake, but his family ordered his body exhumed and brought back to the village graveyard at Leith, Ontario, near their home in Owen Sound. Some believed that this was never done and that Thomson still lay buried in his beloved Algonquin Park.

There was only one way to solve these mysteries and put the rumours to rest once and for all, and that was to exhume Thomson's remains and examine them for signs of foul play. If, contrary to the official records, Thomson was not resting peacefully in his family plot near Owen Sound, his Canoe Lake grave would have to be found and opened.

In the autumn of 1956, four friends from Algonquin Park packed up their knapsacks, gathered a few tools, and decided to do just that.

The men were now digging in a spot not far from where Thomson had drowned. Finding nothing in the first few places they dug, the men took a break and pondered their next move.

Eastaugh wandered over to a rough clearing a few metres away, where his eye spotted a slight, barely noticeable indentation in the ground at the foot of a spruce tree. It was about two metres long and one metre across.

"What do you guys make of this?" he called out.

"Looks like it might have been a grave," Little said as they hurried over.

"Or still is," Gibby added hopefully.

"We should dig here," Braught said as he cleaned off his muddy shovel blade with his boot.

"I agree, but it won't be easy," Little said, indicating the six-metre-tall spruce tree growing in the very centre of the sunken area.

They started digging at one end of the indentation, just to see what they might find. No need to disturb the tree unless they found something, they agreed.

An hour passed as the men worked in silence under a cold drizzle.

"There's nothing here," Gibby said as the rain and sweat dripped down his face. Next to him, a pile of sandy-red earth, roots, and rocks had been growing slowly but steadily as the hole beneath him got wider and deeper.

Then, just as it was starting to get dark, it finally happened.

Five feet down, Little's shovel blade hit something hard. A chunk of it snapped off and he passed it up to the others to examine. They quickly realized it was not another root, but a piece of finished pinewood with a bevelled edge — definitely manmade. "It must be part of a coffin," Eastaugh said, barely able to conceal his sudden excitement.

More wood easily came away, revealing a gaping black hole in the earth — an unmistakeable grave. Little wiped away as much of the surrounding earth as he could and grabbed hold of the wood. It was so decayed that a large portion ripped away without much effort. He carried it out of the hole and held it up to the others.

"At last, we've found it!"

Exhausted, muddy, and now suddenly nervous, the four paused in their work, each of them fully aware of the significance of this moment. They had set out that day with high hopes but limited expectations, armed with forty-year-old information that could very well have been hearsay from the beginning. What they now discovered buried in a hidden grave beneath a nondescript spruce tree could finally prove one of the many theories about Tom Thomson's baffling death.

Gibby couldn't resist any longer. He thrust himself head-first into the hole and reached into the black, hollow space beyond the jagged wall of rotted pine. The next thing his friends knew, he was clambering up out of the grave, triumphantly holding up a brown bone.

Braught produced a flashlight from his knapsack and shone it directly on the bone. "That sure looks human to me!"

"No doubt about it, gentlemen!"

Within seconds, axes were swinging at the roots of the spruce tree. Once it toppled over and was dragged clear, they switched back to shovels and eagerly dug into the damp, sandy earth. The digging seemed to go much easier now that they knew they had found what they had been looking for. Soon they were using their hands instead of shovels, as more and more pieces of finished wood were brought to the surface.

Finally, as the last grey light of late afternoon disappeared, the four men had opened the grave. Lowering their lanterns into the hole, they saw that a coffin had been buried inside a pine box. The lid of this box had rotted and collapsed onto the coffin, which in turn had caved in on the body. As a result, the bones were covered in earth. At this point, it was too hard to tell if there was even an entire skeleton in the coffin.

Gibby's keen eye caught a glint of metal as he moved a lantern. He reached down and pulled up a small plate. Wiping the mud from the smooth surface, he held it to the light to read the engraved message: Rest in Peace.

The men paused solemnly, as if suddenly aware that they had just disturbed a man's grave.

"We're running out of light," Little said. "What should we do?"

"Pulling everything up out of that grave is out of the question," Braught observed, and the others nodded in agreement.

"We'll take this bone right to Dr. Ebbs," Little said. "He's well versed in the Thomson mystery and could identify this bone. If it's Thomson's, he'll be able to tell us." He carefully wrapped it up and placed it in his knapsack.

They could not leave the grave open, so they covered it all with tarpaper, knowing they would be returning later that night or early the next morning.

The four men slapped each other on the back in triumph as they made their way down the hill and set off through the dark, wet woods. They were certain that their discovery in this hidden grave would finally solve the Tom Thomson mystery.

But in fact the mystery was much more complex than any of them could imagine. As it turned out, what they found would only make the whole thing even more baffling.

2

From Forests to Fields

The Thomson family's roots were embedded in the rich Ontario soil long before Confederation. Their history in Canada dates back to the 1830s, with the arrival of the first few plague-infested passenger ships from Europe, most of them carrying immigrants from Scotland and Ireland.

One of the many hopeful young Scotsmen who took the long, harrowing journey across the Atlantic in a crowded ship was Thomas Thomson — a strong, outspoken man in his twenties who had heard glowing tales of wide-open Canada and could not resist the promise of a better life in the New World. With a bit of hard work and determination, he was told, a man could succeed beyond his wildest dreams. And when it came to hard work, no one was more willing to roll up his sleeves and pitch in than young Thomas Thomson, whose reputation as a witty, fun-loving character was long established in the small Scottish town of St. Fergus. He was also known as a bit of a rogue, for it was whispered that he was leaving Scotland to escape the wrath of several young women, at least two of whom had borne him a child. He promised to make good in America and send money home to support the children, but no one really expected to hear from him again.

Relatives and friends throughout his home county of Aberdeenshire had not called him Tom, but instead pronounced his name Tam. He liked the way it sounded, and carried this pronunciation with him on the ship to Canada, where he would be known as Tam for the rest of his life.

Tam Thomson's journey was long and difficult. In those days it was not uncommon for the voyage and immigration process to last four months. Most of the passengers aboard the small, tightly packed ships were poor and undernourished, eager to find a better life in North America. Many of them fell ill with typhus and other deadly diseases during the voyage, but the medical facilities on board were woefully lacking. Some survived their illness, but many died before they reached the mouth of the St. Lawrence River. Every day during the voyage, horrible family tragedies played out right in front of young Tam's eyes; the sights, sounds, and nauseating smells of that dreadful Atlantic crossing would always stay with him.

Luckily, Tam was exceptionally strong. He managed to avoid illness and emerged from Montreal's quarantine shacks with a clean bill of health and a strong determination to succeed in this new land. After so many weeks in the tightly cramped quarters aboard ship, he was anxious to be set free in the fresh air of the open countryside. He had only one disadvantage — he was uneducated in the formal sense — but that only strengthened his will to make good.

"I never filed six-penny worth of paper in any school," was Tam's proud claim whenever asked about his education back in Scotland. Still, he always had a keen appreciation for the value of books and the knowledge they contained. He taught himself to read and was soon considered one of the more cultured and learned men of Pickering Township, east of Toronto, where he bought a few acres of land and settled down to the life of a farmer.

Before long, Tam's hearty nature and quick sense of humour earned him many friends among his fellow pioneers. Whenever his neighbours needed a hand, Tam was there for them, and they gladly returned the favour whenever there was a big job to be done on the Thomson farm. It was easy to like the rugged Scot with the thick accent who loved to recite ancient rhymes and sing the old songs of his homeland while he worked. He was, to all who knew him, an eccentric but loveable local character. An ancient photograph of Tam Thomson shows a squarely built man with chiselled features and chin whiskers, wearing an expression on his face that clearly conveys his unease at having to pose stiffly in a photographer's studio.

Life in Upper Canada was hard. Tam's land was heavily forested and it had to be cleared section by section before he could devote himself entirely to raising crops. Axe blades cut into tree trunks and little by little huge pines and oaks were felled and turned into lumber. Boulders were wrapped in chains and pulled from the ground by teams of oxen. The first seeds were planted in crude rows between tree stumps and rocks. Soon, parts of the wild, rugged forest were transformed into flat, orderly lines of crops. Tam had carved out a piece of the wilderness and claimed it for himself. He even quarried stone from the ground with the hope of one day building a large granite farmhouse.

During those early years, Tam courted an old friend who had come over from Scotland shortly after he had arrived. Elizabeth Brodie, known to all as Betty, was hearty and strong, and would prove to be Tam's ideal partner in his ongoing struggle to tame the wild land and turn forests into fields. Moreover, in an age when the Church played a significant role in everyday life, she was a pious Presbyterian who could provide spiritual support when times got tough — and there were plenty of tough times for farmers working the unforgiving, rugged land.

The couple married in 1839, and Betty moved into Tam's log cabin on the edge of his land. They worked hard together, enduring a freezing cold winter, the loss of livestock to illness and predators, and many other hazards of pioneer life in the harsh Canadian climate. A year after their wedding, Betty bore their first and only child, a son they named John. But Tam had little time to enjoy fatherhood, for there was always more soil to be tilled, more land to be cleared, and a proper house to be built. To make matters worse, Betty fell deathly ill in childbirth and took nearly a year to recuperate. Consequently, the full strength of her youth would never return.

Finally, after several years of struggling against the land, the small farm was flourishing and Tam was able to complete the large farmhouse he had been dreaming of for years. It was an impressive sight — a one-storey house built solidly of grey and rose-coloured granite, with a steeply pitched roof and a huge chimney. The Thomsons moved into these more comfortable quarters, confident that the worst was behind them.

By the time young John Thomson was old enough to attend school, the small town of Claremont was just establishing itself, emerging from the wilderness about a kilometre from the Thomson farmhouse. Aside from a general store, a small inn, and a post office, Claremont also had a large log cabin that served as the local schoolhouse where John learned the rudiments of reading and writing from what was later described as a "succession of drunken schoolmasters."

"You'll have none of that!" was Tam's angry reaction when he caught wind of the poor level of teaching in Claremont. Before he knew it, John was taken out of the local school and enrolled in a much more reputable institution in nearby Whitby. This meant a long, dreary walk every morning and afternoon, but John was as hearty as his father and didn't mind the hardship. Sure enough, the new school opened the young Thomson's eyes to the world of literature, geography, and mathematics. Like his father, he grew to love books and appreciate the power of the written word. But also like his father, he chose not to pursue a career in Toronto, the big city on the lake. He had been born and raised on a farm, he reasoned, therefore the life of a farmer was certainly good enough for him.

"Neckties and ledgers are fine for some men, but I was cut from the land," John told his friends whenever asked about his career ambitions. Despite an education that would be considered superior to most young men in Claremont, John turned his attention to the family farm. More than anything, he preferred the mossy smell of the earth in his nostrils and the feel of the damp soil between his fingers.

To Tam Thomson and his son, John, there was nothing like a relaxing hour or two fishing at a nearby trout stream after a long day of working the land, or a jaunt through the woods on a fine autumn afternoon with their shotguns, their keen eyes and ears alert for signs of small game. They were true outdoorsmen.

* * *

The Thomson farm at Claremont expanded and prospered with both father and son working the land, but it wasn't long before the teenaged John's head was turned by another female presence in the household — Margaret Matheson, a young neighbour Betty had employed to help with the cooking and cleaning. Margaret was a refined local girl who had been born in Ross, Prince Edward Island. She was well-read and shared with the Thomsons a deep appreciation for literature. Her father was a builder by trade; by the time his daughter met John Thomson, he was well known locally as the builder of some of the finest stone homes in the area.

The young couple — John Thomson was nineteen, Margaret just seventeen — were married in Claremont in 1859. The groom's parents' wedding gift was a new house on their property, not far from their own, most likely built by the father of the bride. The new house, set on a bluff overlooking the Thomson farm, was built large enough to accommodate a family, and as the years passed, Margaret bore several children. First came George in 1868, followed by Elizabeth in 1869, Henry in 1871, Louise in 1873, and Minnie in 1875.

By now Tam could claim to be retired. He had long since left the day-to-day running of the farm to John and was content to spend his days idly fishing in the nearby trout streams that he knew so well. The arrival of grandchildren was a great blessing to Tam and Betty, who loved nothing more than to sit back on the porch of their granite farmhouse — built by Tam's own hands from the very rocks in the ground so long ago — and watch this new generation play around the barn and in the fields. For their part, the two oldest children also enjoyed hearing their rugged

Tom Thomson's parents, John and Margaret Thomson, circa 1890. From his father, Thomson inherited a lifelong love of fishing. Both parents instilled in him an appreciation for art and literature.

old grandfather's tall tales and anecdotes of his adventurous youth in Scotland and pioneer life in Upper Canada.

The elder Thomsons did not have much time to enjoy their grandchildren, for it was not long before Betty's health failed again and she died in the summer of 1874. Tam, now frail from so many years of back-breaking labour, lasted just a few months more. He joined his wife up the road in the small Claremont cemetery in March 1875.

With his parents suddenly gone, John lost a vital emotional link to the land he had been born and raised upon. With five children and the recent addition of Margaret's sister, Henrietta Matheson, to the household, even the large farmhouse was getting a bit too crowded for John's comfort.

"I've been considering building a new wing to the house, or possibly moving altogether," John told Margaret one winter day in early 1877. "Five children take up a lot of space."

"Soon to be six," was Margaret's prompt reply, and sure enough by early August the familiar cries of a new baby were heard in the house.

John had waited through Margaret's pregnancy to ensure the safe arrival of his new son, christened Thomas John, but now he was convinced that the best way to accommodate the growing Thomson brood would be to find a larger farmhouse. Leaving his wife in the care of her sister, he packed his wagon and headed north on a quest to scout farms for sale. He spent weeks scouring the back roads of rural Ontario, following up leads in deed offices and reading local newspapers. He visited countless properties, but nothing seemed to suit his requirements. As a farmer he knew exactly what to look for, and if he rubbed the soil between his fingers and did not like what he felt, he promptly moved on.

Finally, John's search brought him farther north to Sydenham Township and an old farm named Rose Hill at Leith, Ontario. It was just a few kilometres outside Owen Sound — an important port town at the foot of the Bruce Peninsula, which separates Georgian Bay from Lake Huron. Rose Hill consisted of one hundred acres, including a big barn and a handsome red brick house with ornate trim around the eaves and, most importantly, plenty of rooms to hold the members of his ever-growing family. He negotiated with the owners and settled on a price of $6,600, and hurried back to Claremont to tell his family to start packing. The Thomsons were moving!

Tom Thomson was just two months old when his family pulled up stakes and left their ancestral home at Claremont for the unknown land up north. At Leith, the big brick house served exactly the purpose John had hoped it would, for the family kept growing to fill its many rooms. Brother Ralph joined the family in 1880. James was born two years later, but he was a sickly baby and survived only nine months. Margaret was born in 1884, and finally Fraser in 1886. The Thomson household now consisted of nine children, two parents, and one aunt; it would have been impossible to house them all comfortably had they stayed in Claremont.

With so many young children running around, the chores required to maintain the large household seemed endless to their mother and Aunt Henrietta, who were kept busy all day, from building fires before dawn to snuffing out candles at midnight. "My sister and I never ate the bread of idleness," was Henrietta's proud claim when she later recalled those difficult first few years at Rose Hill.

John was also kept busy, especially before his eldest son, George, was old enough to take a major hand in the daily chores. The fields at Leith were fertile, and crops grew easily. John continued farming, but after so many years of tilling soil he began to lose interest. He became erratic in his routine and often neglected chores altogether. One year, a neighbour recalled, the fishing was so good that John took his pole down to the creek every day for a few weeks, leaving an entire field of unharvested turnips to rot in the sun.

He also developed an interest in astronomy and took to standing alone on a hilltop, gazing up at the night sky for hours on end — behaviour that did not go unnoticed in the community.

"John Thomson was always regarded as a rather unique character at Leith," another neighbour remembered. "He was a gentleman in every sense, but one of the most eccentric men who ever drew the breath of life."

This was not the only trait John had inherited from his father. A love for books, which John retained throughout his life, was also enough to raise eyebrows in the farming community. This even got him into trouble with his own family on at least one occasion, when he hitched up the horses and drove Margaret into Leith, where she had to do some shopping. To pass the time until she was finished, John dropped into the Leith Public Library, checked out a book, and began reading. He became so wrapped up in the novel that he rushed home to read it through to the end. It was not until much later, when one of the children asked what had become of their mother, that he suddenly remembered — and rushed back into town, bracing himself for the scolding he knew he was about to receive from his stranded wife.

For young Tom, growing up as the sixth child in a steadily expanding family meant a crowded childhood — crowded at the dining room table, crowded in the bedroom (which he always had to share with one or two brothers), and even crowded in church, where the Thomson pew had to accommodate a dozen ostensibly devout Presbyterians of various sizes every Sunday morning. Although John had bought Rose Hill specifically for its large farmhouse, Tom much preferred the outdoors and spent most of his time in the wide-open spaces around Leith, where there were woods to explore, creeks with plenty of fish to catch, and meadows where he could catch snakes or watch deer leap gracefully over log fences.

Even the Leith grammar school had little to offer the boy. He dutifully learned the rudiments of arithmetic and spelling, yet he found the curriculum largely dull and pointless. He was most absorbed by the adventure stories he was given to read — tales of faraway places and deeds of heroism in the face of great adversity. But as with most farming communities of the period, the Leith school based much of its curriculum on agriculture, as most of its students would follow in their parents' footsteps and take over the family farm upon graduation — if in fact they ever bothered to finish school at all. Farming was the lifeblood of the community, and all things agricultural came first in Leith, much to Tom's bitter disappointment.

At home things were quite different, thanks to the family's lifelong appreciation of literature and music. Like her husband, Margaret Thomson was an avid reader who insisted on keeping a well-stocked bookshelf in the home. She also loved music, and encouraged her children to take up instruments. While Tom was growing up, his older brothers played in a Leith band, while he was given a violin and mandolin to master. He managed to coax recognizable tunes out of the instruments, and would retain a love of music for the rest of his life, but as he grew older his real love would emerge — and that was for drawing. His cartoons

The Thomsons' barn in Leith, Ontario. The family moved to this farm, named Rose Hill, soon after Tom's birth in 1877.

and caricatures, rough at first but soon quite accurate and amusing, filled his schoolbooks and loose scraps of paper. Even the old cellar door at Rose Hill would eventually bear some of his more colourful illustrations — and be preserved for years afterwards as the locale of the very first original Thomsons.

One thing Tom inherited from his father and grandfather Tam was a lifelong love of fishing. Each autumn, when John took his boat out onto Georgian Bay to bring in the winter's supply of fish, the only Thomson child he could count on to lend a hand was Tom. Moreover, whenever John decided he had had enough of farming for one day and snuck away for a few hours down at the trout stream, young Tom was usually not far behind, his long fishing pole resting on his shoulder. John's favourite book was Izaak Walton's *The Compleat Angler*, a quirky study of fishing and philosophy written in England more than two hundred years earlier. He had a battered old copy that he often carried in his jacket pocket whenever he set off for an afternoon on the riverbank. If the fish were not biting, he could pass the time by reading long passages from the book, often about the habits of the trout or perch that were at that moment darting around in the dark pools below him. Sometimes, if young Tom were with him, he would read passages aloud to his son:

> The Trout is a fish highly valued, both in this and foreign nations. He may be justly said, as the old poet said of wine, and we English say of venison, to be a generous fish: a fish that is so like the buck, that he also has his seasons; for it is observed, that he comes in and goes out of season with the stag and buck. Gesner says, his name is of a German offspring; and says he is a fish that feeds clean and purely, in the swiftest streams, and on the hardest gravel; and that he may justly contend with all fresh water fish, as the Mullet may with all sea fish, for precedency and daintiness of taste; and that being in right season, the most dainty palates have allowed precedency to him.

At first, Tom did not understand all that his father was reading to him. But as the years went by and he picked up the book to read for himself, he found *The Compleat Angler*'s curious mixture of prose, dialogue, and verse to contain a wealth of wisdom about fishing and life itself. Walton's words became like scripture, the book itself a much more interesting alternative to the Bible — which to Tom was only good for its wide, white margins, begging to be filled in with doodles, caricatures, and quick pencil drawings.

This impiousness on the young Thomson's part led to a running feud with the Reverend J.B. Fraser, minister at the Leith

Presbyterian Church, a large brick building across the road from Rose Hill. A stern, no-nonsense clergyman with piercing eyes and a grey beard, Reverend Fraser was well aware of Tom's growing disdain for the Church, and he went out of his way to call Tom on it whenever possible. Mutual dislike turned to outright hostility one autumn evening when a teenage Tom and a few of his friends were returning home from a long day's work in one of the neighbouring fields. Knowing the regular Wednesday evening prayer service was in progress, Tom suggested they drop in on the proceedings.

"But we're not dressed for it, Tom," said one of his friends.

"Why would the Lord concern Himself with what we're wearing?" Tom replied.

Unable to argue against that reasoning, the others shrugged and followed Tom up the steps of the church. A few seconds later, the doors creaked open and the assembled neighbours and family members cut off their prayers and turned to see Tom and his friends shuffle quietly into a rear pew. Their hair was damp and uncombed, their jackets covered in dust, and their work pants all dirty at the knees. Worse still, they had tracked mud all over the freshly polished church floor.

Reverend Fraser looked up sternly from the pulpit, saw this raggedy addition to his congregation, and cleared his throat. "Gentlemen, that is inappropriate garb for a house of worship!" he bellowed, his eyes fixed on the undoubted ringleader.

Publicly humiliated, Tom vowed that his feud with the local minister would continue unabated. Soon, many of Leith Presbyterian's prayer and hymn books were mysteriously illustrated with unflattering caricatures of a certain bearded minister, often prompting snorts of laughter from an embarrassed member of the congregation during solemn moments of worship.

A while later, when Reverend Fraser was invited to dine at the Thomson home, Tom was asked to help serve. Knowing the minister loved plenty of butter, Tom served him only a small bit at a time, and made himself as annoying as possible throughout the meal, constantly asking if he wanted more butter, which he invariably did. This evoked muted snickers from the siblings around the table, but John and Margaret were livid when they finally caught on to what their son was doing.

But try as he might, Reverend Fraser was never able to herd young Tom Thomson into the Leith Presbyterian Church's flock. After a long week of working in the fields, Sunday was a day of rest — but Tom chose to observe the Sabbath in his own way, fishing or hunting in the surrounding countryside. He rarely set foot in the Leith Presbyterian Church again, and despite his family's close ties to the local church community, Tom would never be on friendly terms with Reverend Fraser.

3

A Young Man About Town

To the adolescent Tom Thomson, Owen Sound was the closest thing to a major city he had ever known. It had stores, restaurants, and waterfront docks where on any given day a dozen big lake steamers were either unloading their cargo or taking on goods bound for other port cities on the Great Lakes.

While he would always be most at home in the quiet woods by a babbling trout stream, there were any number of thrills to be had in the city. He made his way to Owen Sound as often as he could, usually walking the whole way. His heart would start beating rapidly as soon as he spotted the silhouettes of the big dockside grain elevators in the distance, for he knew he would soon be surrounded by bright lights, loud, lively music, and the rowdy company of his friends.

Thomson could now afford the life of a bon vivant, for he was quite wealthy — at least by the standards of any Leith farm boy — thanks to a grandfather he had never known. Tam Thomson's years of hard work paid off and he had died a wealthy man, leaving the sum of twenty thousand dollars to John, which allowed him to buy the larger farm at Leith. Another twenty thousand was to be held in trust and divided among the grandchildren when they came of age. To Tom, Grandfather Tam was just a stern face in the big photo album in the parlour, and the source of strange handwriting in the family Bible. Still, he grew up knowing he had $2,000 coming to him one day — and there was nothing like daydreaming about all the wonderful ways he would spend it.

Just like his older brothers before him, Tom dutifully worked on the Rose Hill farm until he was twenty-one, which was when the Thomson boys were expected to receive their inheritance and begin thinking about making their way in the world. In 1898 he finally received his inheritance and was now a familiar figure on the streets of Owen Sound. It did not take much for any of his friends to talk him into picking up the check at the town's best restaurants or paying for a night out at one of the local dance halls.

Within a year, an alarmingly large portion of the money was gone — spent quickly on expensive shirts, hats and suits, not to mention that treacherous, age-old combination of wine, women, and song. It was a hard lesson in economics, but Thomson could not help living for the moment. He knew all about the wisdom of tucking money safely away in a bank account and not touching it, but that was not for him. Throughout his life, his approach to personal finance would remain simple: If you had money, you spent it; if you didn't have money, you made do with whatever you did have.

One day in the fall of 1899, a group of Thomson's friends decided they had had enough of their quiet, uneventful lives in

Tom Thomson with his brothers and brother-in-law, circa 1905. From left: Tom, Ralph, George, Henry, and Tom Harkness.

Owen Sound and struck upon a sure-fire scheme to drum up some real adventure for themselves. Great Britain was at war with the Boer republics in South Africa, and many Canadian lads were going over to join in the action. After a few drinks in a local tavern to steady their nerves, Thomson and his friends went down to a recruiting office in Owen Sound and presented themselves for service to Her Majesty, Queen Victoria.

The young men were accepted immediately after a brief physical examination, but one of them was turned away.

"Weak lungs," Thomson was told when he demanded to know why he had been rejected.

Outraged that he had been singled out and denied this great adventure, he stormed out of the recruiting office and went straight out in search of a job. *Weak lungs? Damn them and their rules*, he thought. *I'll make my way just fine! I'll show them!*

For Thomson, making his way meant getting a job outside of Leith, and since he was now in Owen Sound every day anyway, that seemed to be the best place to look. Before long he was taken on as a machinist's apprentice at the big Kennedy and Sons foundry. It was hot, dirty work, and the days were so long that he had to leave Rose Hill before sunrise and trudge twelve kilometres to work — then wearily make his way home at dusk. To make matters even worse, he found his coworkers to be a foulmouthed bunch who complained bitterly about their jobs and each other all day long.

"This work is not for me," he would tell anyone who happened to ask him about his new role as a workingman. "I don't suppose I have much of a future as a machinist."

Passing by the foundry's front office one day, Thomson paused by the open door and saw men wearing smart suits and bowties, sitting calmly at desks. They were clean and comfortable, and he heard one of them chuckle merrily in the middle of a friendly conversation.

"Those fellows in the office have it sweet," Thomson told his boss when he returned. "How do you suppose they landed those jobs?"

"They went to school."

"So did I ..."

"They went to college. Accounting and business. That sort of thing. Now get back to work."

Business college! The answer had been right in front of Thomson for several years, but he had not seen it — his brothers George and Henry had not only gone to business college, but George was now a co-owner of a thriving business college in Seattle, Washington.

A quick exchange of letters between Leith and Seattle settled the matter. George had attended the Canadian Business College in Chatham, Ontario, and recommended that Tom enrol there.

Eight months after entering the hot, dark world of the Kennedy foundry, Thomson happily said farewell to his boss and unpleasant coworkers. They could keep their long hours and backbreaking work. If things went according to plan, it would not be long before he could put on a silk shirt and a smart suit each morning and join the ranks of the office clerks — working in a clean, comfortable office all day, puffing leisurely on his pipe as he shuffled papers and joked amiably with his pleasing coworkers. Best of all, he would not be returning home exhausted each night.

At the turn of the century, the Diller Hotel in Seattle, Washington, was one of that city's busiest places. On any given day, a parade of cowboys, lumberjacks, and prospectors on their way to the Klondike passed through its lobby, mixing with travelling salesmen, businessmen, and a colourful array of local characters.

The tall young man who operated the elevator on the evening shift had a front-row seat to it all, overhearing their candid conversations as he went through the repetitive motions of pushing the big brass lever and hauling open the cage-like grill when they arrived at the next floor.

"Every night I get a real education in human nature," Thomson proudly replied whenever asked about his job at the hotel. "A lot of things happen on those four floors, and I see most of it."

The Pacific Northwest was a big change from Owen Sound, but Thomson quickly fell in love with Seattle. It rained a bit too much for his liking, but other than that he felt at home among the thick forests of big fir trees just outside of town, not to mention the bustling docks along the waterfront where he was invigorated by the salty ocean air of Puget Sound.

Thomson had come west in 1901 with one of his Owen Sound friends, Horace Rutherford. He had been encouraged by his brothers to settle in Seattle to study at the Acme Business College, which his brother George co-owned. He had just spent a year in Chatham, Ontario, studying at the Canadian Business College under instructor C.C. Maring, and now had enough basic business training to continue his studies on a more advanced level. He threw himself into his work at the college, attending classes by day, then donning a military-like uniform and reporting for duty at the Diller each evening.

Operating the hotel elevator was good, steady work, but for Thomson it was frustrating. He was used to the wide-open spaces of the Ontario countryside, and was often uncomfortable after spending so much time in a cramped elevator car of just a few square metres. To make matters worse, the sight of some of his passengers — hearty outdoorsmen with the scent of the forest still on them — made him wish he was going with them when they left. They were going places, while he was just going up and down.

Rutherford and Thomson had found rooms at the home of the Shaw family, a sprawling boarding house on Seattle's Twenty-First Street. The company at the Shaws' was always happy and lively, with animated conversations around the big dining room table and Saturday night sing-a-longs around the piano in the parlour. Before long, two more Thomson bothers, Henry and Ralph, arrived in Seattle. Ralph took up lodgings at the Shaws' and was immediately taken with the family's eldest daughter, Ruth. This struck a nerve with Tom, who had yet to find a girl for himself.

Thomson believed that Seattle was the ideal place to settle down and raise a family, especially now that he found himself comfortably in the middle of an Owen Sound gang of friends and close relatives who were intent on putting down roots. He loved the bustling city of tall buildings and clanging streetcars, and his head spun whenever he considered all of its advantages — from its many saloons and quality restaurants to its business opportunities and chances for employment. Motion pictures were still in their infancy in those days, but Seattle was a major stop on several Vaudeville circuits, which meant there were many local theatres offering an entire evening's worth of live musical entertainment for just a few cents.

On his nights off from the hotel, Thomson loved nothing more than to put on a brightly coloured silk shirt with a smart suit and bowtie, take a few drinks with friends at a local watering hole, then spend the rest of the evening at the theatre — laughing at the comedians and humming along with the musical acts. One of Thomson's favourite shows at the time was the hit musical *Floradora*, which he went back to see several times during its long Seattle run. He especially loved one of the songs from the show, "In the Shade of the Sheltering Palm." He memorized the lyrics and would sing it in his clear tenor voice whenever the mood struck him.

But Seattle was still far from idyllic. Thomson was well aware of the city's seedy underbelly of crime and corruption, which he witnessed first-hand at his job in the hotel — and sometimes even found himself an unwilling participant.

Late one night, after his shift at the Diller, he was making his way back to Mrs. Shaw's boarding house when he decided to take a shortcut through a vacant lot. Something stirred in the shadows and he suddenly found himself face-to-face with an unshaven young man who threw him against the damp brick wall.

"Gimme your money — all of it!"

At first, all Thomson could see was the revolver pointed at his chest. It looked just like those he had seen hanging in the holsters of cowboys on his elevator. Then he noticed that the hand holding the gun was shaking violently.

"It's alright," Thomson said calmly. "I have some money in my pocket."

"Make it fast," the young man said, his voice quavering. "And I'll have your watch, too."

Thomson surrendered his pocket watch, then pulled out a few coins and placed them into the robber's shaking hand.

"Now don't move or you'll get it," he warned.

"Just a minute," Thomson said. "You don't seem to be very good at this. Is this your first time?"

The young man before him looked down at his ragged shoes and nodded his head slowly. "You are the first," he admitted. "I have no money and I'm very hungry."

Thomson began searching through his other pockets and came up with two more coins. "Here," he said. "You need this more than I do."

"Thanks, friend," the young man said, snatching the money. Then he straightened up and wielded the revolver threateningly. "Now don't move or you'll get it!" he shouted, disappearing back into the shadows.

The Acme Business College, which occupied a few upstairs rooms in a two-storey building on the corner of Pike Street and Second Avenue, billed itself as place where young men could receive "a bread and butter training in bookkeeping, shorthand, and English." Thomson learned these basics as best he could, but he also took classes in penmanship. Before long he was almost a master of calligraphy, able to handle a fountain pen with ease. He practiced constantly, lettering documents and announcements in a variety of different graphic styles, from plain block letters to fancy flourishes. Most of what he did was intended to prepare him for a career in advertising, providing the handwriting on newspaper ads, signs, and posters.

"This is very good work," George said when he saw his brother's lettering and designs. "I think I might have a job for you."

Two days later, Thomson marched into George's office with a new design — an advertisement for the school's penmanship department.

"Just what we were looking for," George said when Tom presented the document, all professionally composed with illustrations in ink and washes, and, most importantly, several distinctly different styles of lettering.

The work was sent on to a photoengraver, who took Thomson's design and prepared it for publication in a local magazine. Thomson took one look at the photoengraving process and was instantly fascinated.

Meanwhile, the group of expatriate Ontario natives in Seattle continued to grow, and around this time C.C. Maring, Thomson's old teacher from Chatham, had set up shop in the city as a photoengraver. He wasted no time in offering Thomson a job in his new firm, which the young designer eagerly accepted.

Thomson's formal education was now complete. He bade farewell to the Acme Business College and quit his night job at the Diller. He even moved into the Maring home, as his employer offered him a larger room at a cheaper rate than the Shaws. Now

Tom Thomson's business card, announcing him as a commercial designer in Seattle, Washington.

he could officially bill himself as Tom Thomson: Commercial Designer. He even drew a smart business card announcing himself as such, and had a few dozen printed up. For a few weeks thereafter, he proudly distributed one to everyone he met.

Finally, he was a professional!

One of the people who received one of Thomson's business cards was a girl named Alice Lambert, the teenage daughter of a minister and university professor in Portland, Oregon. She was a good friend of Ruth Shaw, and often boarded at the Shaw house on weekends. Thomson spent a lot of his spare time there, visiting his friend Rutherford and brother Ralph, and was still considered part of the Shaws' extended family.

Alice was about seventeen years old — a full nine years younger than Thomson — and he barely even noticed her at first. *She's a just kid*, he thought. But as the weeks went by and he kept meeting her at musical evenings around the Shaw piano, which he and Maring attended each Saturday, the two grew closer.

"Oh, Tom, we must sing 'In the Shade of the Sheltering Palm' again," Alice would urge whenever she felt the atmosphere lagging.

With Maring banging out the chords at the piano, the two would put their heads together and sing in careful harmony:

> My star will be shining love,
> When you're in the moonlight calm...
> So be waiting for me by the eastern sea,
> In the shade of the sheltering palm...
> In the shade of the sheltering palm!

Before he knew it, Thomson was hopelessly smitten. Alice worked as a salesgirl in a millinery shop, selling hats to the city's more affluent women. He found himself turning up at the shop a few minutes before closing time, and they would ride the streetcar together. He could not keep his eyes off her. She was the prettiest girl he had ever met, with blue eyes and delicate Irish features. She was also the most cheerful, giggling every few seconds out of habit, and letting a loud, shrill laugh if something struck her as really funny.

"I swear, Horace, when we sing that song together, she squeezes my hand as if she were singing to me," Thomson confided to Rutherford one Saturday night as they waited for the others in the Shaw parlour.

"Forget it, Tom. She's much too young for you."

Undaunted, Thomson would hear nothing negative about Alice. *He's just jealous*, he thought. *I don't care how young she is ... She loves me!*

Throughout the next year, Alice was Thomson's constant companion. They went on outings together, attended the theatre, and one afternoon he helped her find a house for her parents, who would soon be moving to Seattle from Portland.

There was no doubt about it — they were in love. One evening they found themselves alone in the Shaws' kitchen, and Thomson finally decided to make his move. His heart pounding wildly, he cleared his throat. "Will you marry me, Alice?"

Her mouth dropped open and her eyes widened.

"Well...?"

Alice said nothing. She just stared at him as if he were crazy.

"You act as if you were engaged to someone else," Thomson said after a long, awkward pause.

She giggled nervously, then looked at him with a guilty expression. He was about to ask her what she meant, but she cut him off with a burst of shrill, mocking laughter.

"Rutherford?!" he cried, but she turned away.

Stung, Thomson dropped everything and bolted from the room. The humiliation was too much for him. Soon all of his friends would know what had happened and he would be a laughingstock. *There goes that fool Tom Thomson — he proposed to a girl but she was already promised to his best friend!*

The horrible sound of Alice's mocking laughter rang in his ears as he headed straight back to the Maring house and started packing. *It's all over*, he thought. Within minutes his suitcase was packed and he was thanking Maring for his hospitality.

"You can't just leave, Tom!"

"Yes I can, and I'm going now," he replied, heading for the door. "When is the next train?"

Thomson's departure from Seattle was abrupt and final.

* * *

The tall, lanky figure with the tattered suitcase disembarking at the Owen Sound train station in the autumn of 1905 was coming home a failure. He was twenty-eight years old, and in the past seven years he had not only squandered his inheritance, but had also failed as a soldier, a machinist, a clerk, an engraver and, worst of all, as a suitor.

He hung his head as he made his way slowly to the Thomsons' new home on Eighth Street, which his parents had bought after selling Rose Hill a few years earlier.

"The only things I succeeded at in Seattle were running a hotel elevator and getting held up by a bandit," he complained bitterly to his father. "Perhaps I can make a name for myself as the world's oldest elevator boy by day, and hand over my earnings to street toughs by night."

John Thomson chuckled in spite of himself, then asked about Tom's immediate plans.

"I guess I'll take my drawings down to Toronto and find work in an engraving house," he said. "I've heard there are quite a few of them there."

Sure enough, by the end of the month Thomson was living in a comfortable room in a boarding house on Toronto's Elm Street, and had secured himself a full-time job with Legg Brothers, a photoengraving company with an excellent reputation in the city.

"Have found a job as an artist in a good firm," he wrote home. "It looks like I will be sticking with commercial art and designing."

Most of Thomson's work consisted of drawing and lettering for engraving plates, and he threw himself into his work. He tried not to think about Seattle and its sordid last few hours, but it kept creeping back into his mind. *Should I have acted differently?* he asked himself over and over. *No, I did the right thing.*

Still, every woman he drew somehow turned into Alice. Every time he heard a shrill female voice, he pictured her round face grinning up at him and turning away with a shriek of laughter.

So many times he picked up his pen and began to write her a letter, not sure whether to apologize or demand an explanation. But each time he did, he ended up writing words that would only have reinforced Reverend Fraser's low opinion of him. He crumpled up the paper and tossed it at the wastebasket.

For nearly three years, Thomson quietly took his place in the Legg Brothers' art department each morning and worked on his designs. Before long he was promoted to senior artist, but he had not made friends with any of his co-workers. Worse still, the work was tedious and he hated being cooped up indoors. He daydreamed about fishing while he worked on his designs — and the more he thought about it, the more he yearned to be by the side of a river or out in a boat in the middle of a lake.

This restlessness only got worse, until it reached a point where he found himself looking for any excuse to leave. Then one afternoon he overheard two of his coworkers discussing their wages and complaining how the Legg Brothers were underpaying their staff.

"Why, there are plenty of design firms in Toronto that pay as much as five dollars per week more than the Leggs," one was saying. "I have half a mind to hand in my notice and find another position!"

That was all Thomson needed to hear. He gathered up his papers, put on his coat and hat, and quietly slipped out of the office. It was an impulsive move, but by doing so he was changing the course of his life — and eventually, the course of Canadian art.

4

Shooting the Rapids

One morning in the winter of 1908, Albert "Ab" Robson was in his office at the Toronto commercial design firm of Grip Limited on Temperance Street, when there came a knock at his door.

"Someone here to see you, Ab."

"Show them in."

Robson looked up from his papers as a tall, wiry man in a dark blue serge suit and a grey flannel shirt stepped into his office. He was about thirty years old, Robson judged, with a thin, aquiline nose and black hair combed carefully over his right forehead. He carried a bundle of papers under his arm.

"The name's Thomson," the visitor said quietly, extending his hand. "I was wondering if you had an opening in your art department."

There was something about this Thomson fellow's shy demeanour that Robson liked right away. He seemed humble and unpretentious, unlike many of the arrogant young designers, long on flair but short on talent, who came in badgering him for a job. Robson asked to see examples of Thomson's work, and found himself whistling with satisfaction as he looked over the portfolio.

"That's excellent lettering," he said, pointing to an advertising poster Thomson had created. What Robson was really looking for was a sense of design — the ability to produce a piece of artwork in which all the elements complemented each other. Thomson seemed to have that ability; in each design, the lettering always matched the style of the illustration.

"When can you start?" Robson asked, carefully rolling up Thomson's samples.

Barely two weeks passed before Robson received a telephone call from a man who identified himself as one of the Legg brothers, Thomson's previous employer. "I hear you've hired that Thomson fellow," he said.

"That's right," replied Robson. "What of it?"

"A word to the wise. He's trouble."

"I don't believe it."

"You'll soon see for yourself. He's a very difficult man to work with. His work and behaviour were both erratic and quite unsatisfactory. You would do well to dismiss him before he causes you real trouble."

Robson stuck by his instincts about Thomson. "I still don't believe a word of it," he said, hanging up the phone.

He stood up and walked around to his open office door and looked out at the large room were eight men were sitting at their desks, diligently working on their designs. Thomson was in the furthest corner, completely absorbed in his work, lettering an ornate illustration. Just then, senior designer Jim MacDonald came in from the hall and paused at Thomson's desk. He watched over Thomson's shoulder for a few minutes, like a schoolteacher observing a student, and finally patted him on the back.

"That's fine work, Tom," he said, moving on toward his own desk.

Robson smirked. *Those damned Legg brothers*, he thought. *Always trying to put one over on us!*

There was no question that Thomson was a good commercial artist, for his work was always top-notch as far as Robson was concerned. But there was a dark side of him that came out from time to time. If a design was not going well, Thomson might suddenly let out of gasp of anger, crumple up the paper, and throw it across the room. Perhaps this was what Mr. Legg had warned him about.

The staff at Grip Limited would always remember the day when Thomson's violent temper got the best of him. "A man under the influence of liquor got into the studio and made himself as objectionable as possible," Robson recalled. "Tom tried to continue his work, but when the visitor became personally abusive Tom's slow temper finally rose. He took off his coat and threw the visitor out of the building. The noise of the overturning chairs and tables attracted my attention, but by the time I got there Tom was brushing imaginary dust off his hands and settling back to finish his drawing."

Thomson could not have hoped for a more suitable mentor in the Grip art department than Jim MacDonald, a thin, red-haired man, just a few years older than Thomson but already a highly respected veteran of the commercial art business. Known publicly by his initials J.E.H. MacDonald, he was a quiet, soft-spoken gentleman who had been born in the north of England of Canadian parents and had come to Canada at age thirteen.

Unlike Thomson, MacDonald was a family man with a wife and young son to support, so he often made a few extra dollars by taking on freelance design projects, which he worked on in the evenings and on weekends. Sometimes he needed help in completing an assignment on time and would invite Thomson out to his house in Thornhill to lend a hand. Before long, Thomson was a regular visitor at the MacDonald home, where he got to know MacDonald's wife, Joan, and their son, Thoreau.

The circle of friends and acquaintances continued to grow as more commercial artists joined Grip Limited. In early 1911, a tall, quick-witted Englishman named Arthur Lismer joined the firm, and a few months later Robson hired a talented young designer named Franklin Carmichael. The office boasted a diverse stable of talent in order to provide the widest possible variety of services to its clients, but one thing most of the men had in common was a passion for painting. They had to earn a living by creating art for others, but on Sundays they loved to get together and go sketching on the outskirts of town.

Bill Broadhead, Frank Johnston, Ivor Lewis, Tom McLean, and Ben Jackson — as well as MacDonald, Lismer, and Carmichael — could be counted on to join the fun as picnic baskets and sketching materials were packed up and brought along to the outskirts of town. Their favourite spots were Lambton Mills, where they sketched along the banks of the Humber River, or York Mills on the Don River. These were idyllic Sundays for the Grip men, who would spend lazy hours sketching landscape while their wives and children socialized.

To some, it was simply a pleasant way to spend an afternoon, but to Thomson it was a valuable learning experience. By watching the others, he figured out how to handle oil paint — how to mix colours, how to thin out the paint, and how to capture the essence of the landscape in line and colour. His first few efforts to recreate the scene in front of him were not promising, but MacDonald was unwavering in his encouragement. "Keep at it, my boy," he said. "Think of the overall design."

The rustic landscapes beyond the city limits were fine for casual day trips to sketch the countryside, but it wasn't long before Thomson was yearning to travel much farther afield. This sentiment was shared by several of his Grip colleagues, and in the summer of 1911 he and his office mate Ben Jackson decided to spend their holidays up at Lake Scugog, northeast of Toronto.

They travelled by canoe though the wild country, camping along the way. It had been a long time since Thomson had to chop wood and build a campfire, but the skill returned. He had forgotten how much he missed the wilderness. Even when rain pelted against the side of the tent, he sat contentedly cleaning his pipes and fixing his fishing lures. Best of all, the trip offered Thomson a chance to sketch every day, and his work progressed rapidly. Dark clouds looming over even darker lakes, scraggy spruce trees, and driftwood. His brush moved quickly across the wooden panel to capture the scenes he and Jackson encountered as they paddled.

Thomson was hooked. The Lake Scugog trip was so invigorating that he vowed to return as soon as he could, but he never made it back there. Instead, on the recommendation of their Grip colleague Tom McLean, he and Jackson decided to try another sketching ground the following spring — a place called Algonquin Park, a huge reserve of lakes, rivers, and forests between Georgian Bay and the Ottawa River.

Of course Thomson could not have known it at the time, but when he and Jackson stepped off the train at Canoe Lake station on a bright evening in May 1912, he was entering a world that would serve as his real home for the rest of his life.

The Algonquin Park landscape was stunning. The two artists paddled down Canoe Lake to Tea Lake and set up their camp near the dam where the lumber companies drove logs through the narrow opening, sending them crashing into the rushing river below. Thomson was struck by the colours and compositions that seemed to present themselves wherever he looked. From tall black spruce trees to steep hills and broad, majestic lakes, he and Jackson were kept busy as they paddled and sketched all day, their fishing lines dragging in the water in wait for supper to strike at their hooks.

"This is a wonderful place," Thomson marvelled as he studied a map of the park. "According to this, you can get around completely by canoe. All the lakes seem to be connected by rivers, or a short portage here and there."

Moreover, the local characters were both colourful and friendly. Shannon Fraser, who owned Mowat Lodge, was also the local postmaster and he held several other positions within the tiny, tightly knit community. He always wore a suit and tie, even if he was chopping wood or cleaning a string of fat trout. Mark Robinson and Bud Callighen were two of the local rangers whose main job was to keep an eye out for fur poachers in the park. Then there was Larry Dickson, a guide who lived in a tiny shack amidst a stand of birch trees, who earned money during the slow seasons by poaching furs when Robinson and Callighen weren't looking.

Thomson and Jackson did not go unnoticed. Sketching was not a common activity in remote Canoe Lake, and Mark Robinson had to admit that of all the ruses and disguises poachers had pulled on him over the years, none had ever tried passing themselves off as artists.

"You better keep an eye on those odd-looking fellows," he was told one day by a local man who pointed at Thomson and Jackson as they walked past. "Yesterday I seen them poking at pieces of wood with little brushes."

"It's okay, they're artists," Robinson replied.

"Artists? What kind of things are they?"

By 1912, anyone who had anything to do with the arts in Toronto knew about the Arts and Letters Club, the unofficial headquarters of the city's creative life. Since its founding a few years earlier, the Club served as a daily meeting place for all the most prominent painters, illustrators, sculptors, writers, actors, musicians, and newspaper critics. Here they mingled with wealthy businessmen and patrons of the arts in a large dining room that was as elegant as it was inaccessible.

Situated in what was once a municipal courtroom at Adelaide and Court Streets, the Club had its only entrance at the end of a dark, damp, and foul-smelling alley behind police headquarters, where members had to step carefully between piles of horse manure and firewood. Mandatory admission to the Club was a log for the fireplace, taken from the woodpile and carried upstairs. Naturally, Robson and MacDonald were avid members of the Arts and Letters Club, where they regularly ate lunch and fraternized with their fellow artists.

It was during this period that MacDonald met and formed a close friendship with Lawren Harris, a wealthy young artist who, as an heir to the Massey-Harris farm equipment fortune, did not have to worry about labouring in the front-line trenches of commercial art. Unlike many of the roughly hewn designers they had known, Harris was elegant and well-spoken. He favoured tailored linen suits and his frizzy hair was always perfectly groomed. Because of his family's wealth, he devoted himself entirely to painting, and was at this time particularly interested in portraying on canvas Toronto's dingy Ward district — the complete opposite to the elegant, tree-lined neighbourhoods in which he was raised.

MacDonald found a kindred spirit in Harris, and together they sketched urban life in Toronto. In the winter of 1912, they went out together and sketched the old gas works. Each ended up painting a large canvas from their sketches. Harris created a haunting image of the large gas tank, seen through a haze of fog and steam, while MacDonald set the tank in the background of his image of steam engines and lumber yards. These paintings drew a lot of attention at the Arts and Letters Club, where fellow artists admired the way Harris and MacDonald had handled the many different shades of snow in their urban scenes.

One of these admirers was the gregarious Dr. James MacCallum, a well-known eye specialist who was instantly recognizable by his shiny bald head and a large moustache which he kept carefully waxed. He loved the great outdoors and was a keen collector of landscape art. This passion had drawn him into the Arts and Letters Club, where he regularly joined in the discussions and arguments about art — and did so with so much fervour that any new member who did not know him would have assumed he was an artist himself.

Dr. MacCallum fell in easily with Harris and MacDonald. Soon they were regular tablemates at lunch, where Dr. MacCallum kept encouraging his new friends to paint. He invited them to stay at his Georgian Bay cottage, and offered to organize exhibitions of their work at the Arts and Letters Club.

"There are a lot of talented artists right here in Toronto," said Dr. MacCallum.

"Yes, and a great many of them are working with me at Grip," MacDonald replied. "There is one chap who shows great promise — Thomson his name is."

"You must bring him around to the Club," Dr. MacCallum said. "I'd very much like to meet this Thomson fellow."

"You'll have to wait — he's off on another canoe trip through the north country."

At that moment, Thomson was in fact nearly three hundred kilometres northwest of Toronto, paddling a canoe along the choppy Mississagi River above Lake Huron. This time his companion was another fellow Grip artist, Bill Broadhead. Again, they had heard about the unspoiled wilderness of the Mississagi Forest Reserve from their friend Tom McLean, who had been up through there eight years earlier and had described it as the trip of a lifetime.

"But are you sure both of you can handle a canoe properly?" McLean had said before they left Toronto. "That river can get rather tricky in spots."

"Of course we can," Thomson replied quickly, frankly a bit insulted by McLean's needless warning. After all, this would be his third canoe trip.

There would be plenty of opportunities to sketch, McLean promised, but Thomson had a better idea. Not only would he bring his sketch box and panels, but he would also bring a camera and take photographs of the landscape — it was faster and more efficient, he reasoned, plus it would also allow him to take snapshots of any wildlife they encountered along the way.

Weighed down by their tent, blankets, art supplies, and fishing gear, they checked their canoe into a baggage car and took the train north, past Sudbury, to Biscotasing. The next day they set off in their five-metre-long Peterborough canoe, a slender model designed more for speed than stability. They spent the next few weeks paddling through the intricate system of lakes and rivers, carrying their gear over portages and crossing swampy marshes in their long trek south to Lake Huron. They sketched and fished, and Thomson took so many photos that he soon ran out of film and stashed the exposed rolls safely in his gear.

Everything was going well until one day about a month into their trip. The rain was falling and both men were wet and tired.

"I'm not sure I like the look of these rapids," Thomson said as they started moving much faster.

"I'm sure it slows down just around the bend!" Broadhead said hopefully.

But instead of slowing down, the current increased. The narrow, overloaded canoe hurled around the bend with both men paddling frantically to keep from tipping over. Soon the river was just black and white — black rocks jutting up from white foam — and the roar of the rapids was so loud that their shouts were lost in the chaos. Thomson ducked as they shot under an overhanging tree trunk and the bow lurched up sharply, drenching him in icy water. Avoiding the big rocks took split-second timing with the paddle, but even his strong, lightning-fast strokes were useless against the powerful current. Unable to take his eyes off the water ahead, Thomson could not to look back to see how Broadhead was managing. All he could do was try to keep the canoe pointed between the rocks.

Are you sure both of you can handle a canoe properly? Tom McLean's voice echoed in Thomson's head as he struggled against the current. *That river can get rather tricky in spots!*

"Thank you very much, Tom!" Thomson shouted, but the roar of the water completely drowned out his voice.

Then it happened.

The river ahead of them suddenly fell away, and the canoe followed the water downward. Neither man had time to react. They were thrown over a small, violent waterfall and plunged into the churning white rapids. Camping gear, fishing rods, knapsacks, blankets, food, sketching supplies — everything flew out of the overturning canoe and was carried off by the current. Thomson and Broadhead were at first stunned by the freezing cold water, but they managed to keep their heads above the surface. Swimming was useless — they had to let the current propel them through the rapids until they could get a firm hold on one of the slippery rocks.

Once they both made it safely to shore, they had to spend the rest of the day roaming far downriver, searching for their gear in the pools and against the rocks. Thankfully, the canoe was not damaged, but most of what they could salvage from the water was useless. Thomson was able to rescue about a dozen of his sketches, which he found bobbing against the shore.

"This is some fix we're in," Broadhead muttered as they attempted to put up a sopping wet tent as it began getting dark. They had lost the poles in the river, and were forced to cut tree branches as a replacement. What little food they had recovered was soggy and inedible, their blankets were drenched, and there were no dry matches to start a fire. To make matters worse, the steady drizzle showed no sign of letting up, ruling out any hope of anything drying overnight.

"You know, Bill — all things considered, I'd rather be here right now, all wet and cold, than cooped up in some office somewhere."

"I'd settle for a dry office," Broadhead replied, and they both burst out laughing.

"Seriously, the only thing that bothers me is that we lost a few dozen rolls of film," Thomson said after the laughter subsided. "I took some fine photographs back there, and now they're all lost."

The Grip Limited office was a busy place, with any number of clients, designers, suppliers, and messengers hurrying back and forth through the front doors all day, with no one taking much notice of each other. But one afternoon in late summer, when a tall, unshaven man strolled in from the street, everyone suddenly stopped whatever they were doing to stare at him. He wore a long buckskin coat over a red flannel shirt, and leather moccasins that resembled tall boots. On his head was a big woollen tuque, pulled low over his eyes.

The mysterious stranger lurched forward, weighed down by a huge, bulging knapsack strapped to his back. Some people thought he looked like a character from one of the silent adventure movies playing in the nickelodeon down the street. Others assumed he was there to have his photograph taken for an advertisement.

But for the designers at Grip Limited, there was no mystery. As soon as they saw him, they knew it was Tom Thomson, just back from a two-month canoe trip up North. He had come straight from the train station, eager to unwrap his bundle of fresh sketches and spread them out to finish drying.

"You've not heard the news, have you, Tom?" MacDonald said as he moved aside some papers to make room for Thomson's wet panels. "Ab's left Grip. He's now over at Rous and Mann, over on York, in charge of the art department. What's more, he's asked me to go over as well, as head designer."

"We're all considering joining him over there," added Lismer.

"Jumping ship?" Thomson asked. "The whole staff?"

"Call it what you will. Rous and Mann pays seventy-five

cents per hour," said Fred Varley, one of Lismer's friends from England who had recently joined Grip. "You'd jump ship, too!"

"Maybe I will."

Sure enough, by the end of the following week, Thomson was an employee of Rous and Mann Press Limited. So many of the Grip artists had come over with Robson that it was almost as if Grip had simply moved its offices to York Street.

The canoe trips through the northern Ontario forests had awakened something deep down in Thomson that he had not felt so strongly since his boyhood days in Leith — a passion for the wilderness. He knew he had to earn his living in the city, but the call of the North was too loud to ignore.

When Robson, MacDonald, and the others came into work one morning, they were met with a sight none of them would soon forget. There was Tom Thomson, sitting quietly at his desk, concentrating on some papers in front of him. This was not unusual, but on the floor next to him was a huge tub he had borrowed from the photographic department and filled with water. He held a canoe paddle, and was calmly paddling the water while he read. Looking up at the curious expressions all around him, he simply shrugged and said, "I have to practise. They say the paddle shouldn't make a sound if you're doing it right."

But Thomson's love of canoeing was not the only thing that attracted the attention of his fellow workers, for his recent oil sketches were being shown around the office by MacDonald, who believed they showed great potential.

"You should work some of these up onto canvas," Ab Robson said, looking over the small wooden panels depicting colourful lakes under big, expressive skies.

"Oh, I'm very busy," Thomson replied, trying to downplay the attention. "Besides, I don't have the space for an easel at home." This was true, for his boarding house room was barely large enough for a bed, dresser, and chair.

"Sorry, Tom, you'll have to try harder than that," Robson replied, shaking his head. "I'll give you a set of keys to the office and you can come in here on Sundays to paint." He indicated an empty corner where an easel could be set up.

Trapped, Thomson grinned sheepishly and nodded.

For the next few Sundays, Thomson dutifully turned up at the Rous and Mann office and took his place at an easel in the corner. With his pipe clenched firmly in his teeth, he worked diligently on a large canvas, using thick, wide brushstrokes to depict the rocky shore of a choppy, dark blue lake under a brooding grey sky. He filled the foreground with the branches of dead trees jutting out between the smooth brown rocks, giving the scene a rough, untamed look. Knowing that only old-fashioned artists took great care to hide their brushstrokes in an effort to render their paintings as realistically as possible, Thomson applied the paint generously, making sure that each of his brushstrokes stood out on its own.

The final product, which Thomson titled simply *A Northern Lake*, remained on the easel for all to admire throughout much of the winter. He doubted if he could sell it, and was unsure of what to do with it.

MacDonald soon came up with the perfect solution. In the early spring of 1913, the Ontario Society of Artists held its annual exhibition, and MacDonald insisted that Thomson submit *A Northern Lake*.

"It's not good enough," he protested, but MacDonald would hear nothing of it.

"It's far better than most of the old-fashioned drivel they show year after year," he said. "This is true. It embodies the very spirit of Canada."

Thomson took this as a great compliment, for lately MacDonald had been engaging his fellow designers in discussions about Canadian artists expressing the spirit of their native land through landscape painting. Much of this was inspired by a trip MacDonald had recently taken with Lawren Harris down to Buffalo, New York, where they saw an exhibition of Scandinavian art at the Albright Gallery. The two artists had come back to Toronto glowing with inspiration, for they had seen how the cold, wintery landscapes of Norway and Sweden — which, they noticed, bore a striking resemblance to Canada — had been handled by the Scandinavian painters.

"They paint their own land in their own style, expressing the very spirit of their country in a way no one else could," MacDonald said. "That is precisely what we should be doing here in Canada." And so, fired up by MacDonald's enthusiasm to paint Canadian subjects in a way that was uniquely Canadian, many of the Rous and Mann artists submitted their canvases to the Ontario Society of Artists' show. Thomson dutifully sent *A Northern Lake* along with them.

In late April 1913, after the exhibition ended, MacDonald arrived in the office one afternoon with a bundle of framed canvases, all wrapped neatly in brown paper and tied with string. "I've just been by to collect my entries in the OSA exhibition," he said to Thomson. "While I was there, I took the liberty of collecting your *Northern Lake* as well."

"Thanks, Mr. MacDonald …"

"But it wasn't there."

"Wasn't there?"

"No, but they asked me to give you this instead," he said, unable to suppress a wide grin. He reached into his coat pocket and handed Thomson an envelope.

Thomson tore it open and found a letter folded around a cheque. "It says *A Northern Lake* was purchased by the Ontario Government for ... two hundred and fifty ..."

"Congratulations, my boy!" MacDonald said, clapping Thomson on the back. "Well done!"

By now the rest of the staff had gathered around Thomson.

"Atta boy, Tom!"

"The drinks are on Thomson tonight!"

Robson made his way through and shook Thomson's hand. "This is wonderful news, Tom! You'd better take the rest of the afternoon off to go cash that cheque. You'll have plenty of thirsty friends on your hands tonight!"

Flush with triumph and surprise, Thomson carefully pocketed the cheque and headed straight to the bank. He expected the teller to marvel at such a large amount, but he simply took it and stamped the back.

"Will you want all of that in cash, or would you care to deposit it?"

Thomson was suddenly struck with a delicious idea. "No, I'll take it all in cash, please."

"Very good, sir."

"In one-dollar bills."

"I beg your pardon ..."

"I want it all in ones ... Singles ... Dollar bills."

The teller looked at him as if he were crazy. After a long pause to make sure Thomson was not just pulling some practical joke, he snorted and went off to the vault. A few minutes passed before he returned, a peeved expression on his face. Dumping two handfuls of neatly stacked dollar bills on the counter, he pushed them toward Thomson. "Two hundred and fifty dollars… Shall I count it all for you, sir?"

"That won't be necessary, my good man," Thomson said, clearly pleased with himself. He strutted out of the bank, already thinking about the fancy silk shirts and painting supplies he would now be able to buy. But first, he headed straight to his boarding house, went up to his room and closed the door.

Finally alone, Thomson took the money out of his pockets and tossed it all up to the ceiling. The tiny room was suddenly filled with a blizzard of fluttering money as Thomson fell onto his bed and let it all float down around him. *The Ontario government bought my painting! I may make a go of this after all!*

That night, as Thomson was going out to meet his Rous and Mann colleagues at a local tavern to celebrate his big sale, he paused at the telephone near the foot of the boarding house stairs and placed a long-distance call home to Owen Sound.

"I sold a painting!" he shouted into the receiver as his parents and Aunt Henrietta gathered around the new phone in the Thomson home. As he spoke, he was reminded of an old feud and could not help but take a good-natured poke at a favourite nemesis. "Oh, and by the way," he said before hanging up, "be sure to tell old Reverend Fraser that I painted it on a Sunday!"

5

Storm Clouds on the Horizon

Thomson was usually very tired after spending a long day at his desk at Rous and Mann, where most of his work consisted of carefully lettering labels and posters for the firm's clients. He took pride in doing a good job each time, but no matter how hard he worked on a design or produced paragraphs of intricate calligraphy, he rarely received a word of praise from clients. It was a thankless job, and he was usually glad to grab his coat and hat at the end of the day and walk all the way from York Street to his room in a big old house on Isabella Street.

Late one evening in the autumn of 1913, Thomson trudged home after an especially exhausting day. As he wearily climbed the steps to his attic room, he noticed that his light was on and his door was slightly ajar. Alarmed, he leapt up the remaining stairs and threw open the door. There, sitting on the bed, was a bald man with a long moustache.

"Finally, Tom!" he cried. "I've been waiting three quarters of an hour!"

It was Dr. James MacCallum, that friend of Lawren Harris from the Arts and Letters Club. Thomson had met him once or twice through Jim MacDonald, but didn't recognize him right away in the unlikely setting of his dimly lit room. The last place he expected to find one of Toronto's leading oph-thalmologists and patron of the arts was in a seedy rooming house attic.

"I've been looking over these sketches," Dr. MacCallum said, indicating the collection of Thomson's latest panels that lay scattered around him on the bed and floor. "I am very interested in them."

"Oh, you can take them all home with you," Thomson replied, still startled by the sudden presence in his room. "They're not very good."

"On the contrary! They show great promise."

Dr. MacCallum never apologized for going through Thomson's personal items in his absence. Instead, he complained that Thomson was indeed a hard man to find. MacDonald had directed him to Isabella Street, but couldn't recall the exact address. This left Dr. MacCallum with no choice but to ring the doorbell of every boarding house on the street until he finally found the right one. Then he had to convince Thomson's incredulous landlady that although her tenant was not home, he had to meet with him on a matter of grave urgency and insisted on being let into his room to wait.

"Do you know about the studio we're putting up in Rosedale?" Dr. MacCallum asked.

"Of course," Thomson replied. "It's all that Harris and MacDonald have been talking about. What of it?"

"Well, let me make you a little deal, Tom. I'll personally guarantee your expenses for a year if you devote yourself to painting. You can live in the Studio Building and I will buy or find buyers for all the work you produce."

It certainly was a momentous offer. Thomson quickly realized that if nothing else it meant that he could spend much more time up in Algonquin Park and not have to worry about working long hours on designs for other people. He could be his own boss. His mind began racing with images of himself paddling a canoe across the mirror-like surface of a wilderness lake, dropping a fishing line into a deep pool at the side of a rushing river, and snowshoeing through a silent birch forest. But then he realized that an ironclad commitment to painting might ruin it for him. He painted for pleasure and had never thought to make it his life's work.

"I'll have to think about it," he said finally.

The buzz around the Arts and Letters Club that fall was dominated by news of the Studio Building construction project that Harris was financing with some help from Dr. MacCallum. Second to that was talk of the rising young star named Tom Thomson, who had only recently begun to paint but had already succeeded in capturing the spirit of the northern landscape in the relatively few works he had produced so far.

But by mid-November there was a new name being repeated throughout Toronto's art circles — Alex "A.Y." Jackson. No relation to Thomson's sketching and canoeing companion Ben Jackson, this was a Montreal artist who had studied in France and was now trying his luck in Toronto.

"You should see what this Jackson chap is doing with Canadian themes," Jim MacDonald was saying.

Photo by Karen Forbes Cutler. Collection of the author.

The Studio Building still stands, virtually unchanged, on Severn Street in Toronto. Tom Thomson and A.Y. Jackson were its very first tenants, moving into a ground-floor studio in early 1914 while the building was still under construction.

Thomson was already familiar with Alex Jackson's work, or at least one particular painting entitled *The Edge of the Maple Wood* — a bright, shimmering canvas painted on a crisp spring day in rural Quebec. It had been exhibited earlier that year in the Ontario Society of Artists annual spring exhibition in Toronto, where it immediately drew the attention of MacDonald, Thomson, Harris, and Arthur Lismer. "I can remember this one canvas," Lismer wrote many years later. "It stood out among the usual pictorial array of collie dogs, peonies, and official portraits, like a glowing flame packed with potential energy, and loveliness."

The enthusiasm generated by this single work had prompted MacDonald to send a letter off to Montreal, and soon Jackson was in Toronto to meet what he believed might be a group of kindred spirits. He later went off to spend the summer and autumn up at Georgian Bay, but now he was living and working in Harris's studio above the Bank of Commerce at the corner of Yonge and Bloor Streets. It was here, in late November, that Dr. MacCallum brought Thomson to meet the illustrious artist everyone was talking about.

Thomson didn't know what to expect. As he and Dr. MacCallum climbed the stairs to Harris's studio he grew so nervous that he could barely speak. A well-known artist who had studied in France and had spent a few years painting in Europe — how would he react to a country boy with nothing but a few simple sketches of northern Ontario? To make matters worse, Dr. MacCallum had insisted that Thomson bring along a few of those sketches to show Jackson. He dreaded the very thought of that and, hoping Dr. MacCallum would forget about them, kept his bundle hidden under his jacket.

He need never have worried.

The door opened to reveal a sturdily built young man with white-blonde hair and a big smile. "Any friend of Jim's and Dr. MacCallum's ..." Jackson greeted Thomson in a deep, booming voice that resonated through Harris's studio.

There was no ice to break. Jackson's easygoing personality and self-effacing sense of humour quickly put Thomson at ease, and soon the two were chatting away like old friends. "He was a very likeable fellow," was Jackson's first impression of Thomson. "You just took to him right away. He was rather shy and was almost afraid to show the sketches that he had with him. They were very honest."

Dr. MacCallum was eager for Thomson to see Jackson's work-in-progress, a large, garishly coloured study of Georgian Bay rocks and spruce trees that had lately been attracting a lot of curious attention among the Toronto artists. Sure enough, it was like nothing Thomson had ever seen. Instead of trying to render everything as realistically as possible — surely the goal of every good artist, Thomson thought — Jackson had deliberately redesigned the fir trees to look like scraggly green cones. Now he was adding dashes of violet to the blue sky.

"This is quite commonly done over in Europe," Dr. MacCallum said, seeing the look of surprise on Thomson's face. "But see how it's more rugged, more Canadian."

"Jim MacDonald calls this one *Mount Ararat* because it puts him in mind of the high ground where Noah's Ark came to rest," Jackson said with a chuckle.

Mount Ararat — or *Terre Sauvage*, as it would eventually be titled, took several weeks for Jackson to complete. It was an experimental work that developed on the canvas, which meant that Jackson would rework certain parts of it as new ideas came to him. Over the next few days, Thomson would drop by the studio after work to watch the painting's progress. He stood behind Jackson, puffing his pipe and asking questions about colour and brush strokes as the radical *Terre Sauvage* slowly took shape on the canvas.

Before long, the two most promising landscape artists in Toronto were the best of friends. Jackson told Thomson how Dr. MacCallum had made him the same offer of a year's financial support if he devoted himself to painting. But instead of ringing all the rooming house doorbells along Isabella Street as he did to find Thomson, Dr. MacCallum had searched the islands of Georgian Bay in his motorboat until he found Jackson's camp. Facing an uncertain future and dreading the thought of returning to a commercial art job, Jackson considered the offer a godsend. "Of course I accepted on the spot," he told Thomson.

"I didn't. I turned him down."

"Now that won't do, Tom."

"I don't think I'm ready. I'd only make a damn fool of myself."

"Nonsense. You must go to MacCallum and tell him you've changed your mind!"

"I won't."

Jackson knew he had his work cut out for him. He had heard from the other artists that Thomson could be incredibly stubborn, so over the next few days he kept turning up at Thomson's boarding house, always being sure to bring up the subject of Dr. MacCallum's offer. "You must accept it," he kept repeating.

Finally, when Thomson could take it no more, he threw up his hands in defeat. "Fine! Yes! I'll go see him tomorrow!"

From that day on, Tom Thomson was a full-time landscape painter. His decision could not have come at a better time.

By the end of 1913, most of Thomson's artist friends, especially Lawren Harris, Jim MacDonald, Arthur Lismer, and now Alex Jackson, were eagerly discussing and promoting what they saw as a national art for Canada — a landscape-based modern style that expressed the spirit of the country. Jackson had certainly succeeded in doing that with his *Terre Sauvage*, but there was a price to be paid for being so radical, and everyone sensed there was trouble ahead.

The first blow was struck in the pages of the *Toronto Star*. A small collection of colourful Georgian Bay sketches painted by Jackson a few weeks earlier had been exhibited on the walls of the Arts and Letters Club, where they attracted a lot more attention than anyone expected, especially Jackson himself. The critic F.H. Gadsby took great exception to Jackson's work, which he considered terribly offensive to anyone with conservative tastes in art. The resulting article, titled "The Hot Mush School," attacked the modern artists and their garish work. "All their pictures look pretty much alike," Gadsby wrote, "the net result being more like a gargle or gob of porridge than a work of art."

Knowing that even bad publicity can be good for an artist, Jim MacDonald fanned the flames by composing a stinging rebuttal to Gadsby's article, which the *Star* published the following week. Gadsby's review, MacDonald wrote, "got my goat, my horse, my ass, and everything which is mine." He then got to the main point of his article, which was to promote the notion of a uniquely Canadian art movement. "Let us support our distinctly native art, if only for the sake of experiment," he wrote, hoping to stir up more controversy. The more attention they received in the press, the more people would be interested in viewing their work — if only to see what all the fuss was about.

The battle was on!

Finally, after more than a year of long discussions around tables in the Arts and Letters Club and countless consultations with architect and contractors, the Studio Building was finally near completion.

Harris and Dr. MacCallum were at the Severn Street site nearly every day, eagerly anticipating the moment when the construction foreman would tell them that the last baseboard had been nailed in and the last wall painted. As it turned out, the artists were so eager to get started that the moment never came. Instead, in January 1914, one of the studios on the ground floor was deemed ready enough to be occupied, so Jackson was invited to vacate Harris's studio and move in, while Thomson was advised to give notice at his boarding house. Dr. MacCallum's two beneficiaries would be the first occupants of Studio One.

Even while still in the final stages of construction, the Studio Building was an impressive sight, and it would be a source of great pride to Harris for many years to come. It was a square, three-storey red brick building of the most modern design. The location had been well chosen, for Severn Street was not only a very quiet spot on the edge of Rosedale Ravine, but also a convenient five-minute walk from the corner of Yonge and Bloor Streets. Inside, the six studios were large and airy, with high ceilings and a small gallery in the rear for storage. The north wall of each studio was dominated by a huge window overlooking Severn Street. A northern exposure was considered ideal for an artist's studio because it was always even, with no direct sunlight to cast shifting shadows across the room.

The first month in the new studio was anything but quiet. Between them, the two artists had little in the way of luggage or furniture — just a few books and their painting supplies — so the cavernous, empty studio resonated with hammering, sawing and other loud construction noises all day long as work continued on the unfinished studios upstairs.

"We had much to talk about," was how Jackson later recalled those early days in Studio One with Thomson. "He would tell me about canoe trips, wildlife, fishing, things about which I knew nothing. In turn, I would talk to him of Europe, the art schools, famous paintings I had seen, and the Impressionist school which I admired."

Thomson also surprised his roommate with his reading habits. He was a member of the local library and was constantly heading out to borrow and return books. If a book caught Thomson's interest, Jackson noticed, he would stay up all night to read it through to the end — a trait he had inherited from his father.

Since neither had a source of income other than Dr. MacCallum's financial support, they had to keep their daily expenses down to a bare minimum. They normally worked all day, pausing only to go out for a sandwich and coffee at a nearby restaurant called the Busy Bee, or to a bar over on Yonge Street that served hot meals for just twenty-five cents. This suited the gregarious Jackson, but Thomson did not always like going out. He was always complaining that the studio had not come equipped with cooking facilities — not even a hotplate — for he loved preparing simple but hearty meals, regardless if he was far out in the bush or right in the middle of the city.

For entertainment, they would attend a play or a musical recital at the Arts and Letters Club, or perhaps take in a silent movie at one of the many cinemas that were popping up all over Toronto. All the while, as they were walking along the street or sitting down to a meal, Thomson kept Jackson entertained with stories and vivid descriptions of his favourite sketching ground — Algonquin Park.

One day, while looking through Thomson's sketches, Jackson found a lively image of moonlight shimmering across a lake. "This is very Impressionistic," he said as Thomson gasped in disbelief at his own abilities. "You ought to work this up onto a large canvas."

Before Thomson could even protest, a blank canvas was placed on his easel and Jackson was searching through his art books for an example to illustrate his point. Sure enough, he found a reproduction of night painting by Dutch artist Vincent van Gogh. Running his paint-stained finger across the page, Jackson showed Thomson how van Gogh had used short, forceful brush strokes of white and yellow to form swirling patterns of light in the evening sky.

Soon Jackson was standing behind Thomson as he blocked in an Algonquin Park lake under a bright half moon. The composition was different than those of most landscape painters, but it was already a Thomson trademark — water and distant shore very low down on the canvas, with the vast majority of space devoted to the sky above.

"Don't paint it too dark," Jackson advised. "It may be night time, but there's still a lot of light in the sky."

Thomson knew exactly what his friend meant. Soon the dark sky was ablaze with dashes of yellow moonlight. He made circular motions with his brush, creating a halo around the moon, and then he added generous dabs of bright reflections on the surface of the calm lake below. When he was finished, the only dark space left on the canvas was the silhouette of forest along the distant shore. The rest was a carefully composed arrangement of light. He lit his pipe and gazed thoughtfully at the canvas.

"It's very modern," he said after a long pause. "It looks European, like in your books, but at the same time it's very … Canadian."

"That's the idea," Jackson said brightly. "We can learn a few tricks from our European cousins and apply them to our own country."

Thomson was not so sure. It all sounded simple enough when Jackson spoke about it, but he knew he had a long road ahead of him if he was going to learn modern techniques. After this short time with Jackson, his head was spinning from all the new ideas and theories he had never heard of a few weeks earlier.

* * *

Jackson awoke one morning bubbling over with enthusiasm. "Let's go, Tom!"

"Where?"

"Algonquin Park! You keep talking about it, and now I can't wait to see it for myself, so let's go ... today!"

Thomson's answer surprised him. "I'm not ready. I still need to work on these canvases. Besides, they might have some work for me at Rous and Mann next week, and the money will come in handy. You go on up by yourself, and I'll be up in a few weeks."

Late that night, Jackson may have regretted his sudden decision to leave the comforts of the Studio Building for the remote wilderness of Algonquin Park — in the middle of winter. After a twelve-hour train trip up through the snowy north country, he found himself standing alone on the platform of the Canoe Lake station, weighed down by his luggage of painting supplies and snowshoes. To make matters worse, it was cold — much colder than anything he had ever experienced.

Back in Toronto the next day, Thomson received a tersely worded telegram:

ARRIVED CANOE LAKE LAST NIGHT 40
BELOW ZERO

As it turned out, Jackson's stay at Algonquin Park proved to be pleasant and successful. He quickly got to know most of the locals — including Shannon Fraser at Mowat Lodge, and the rangers Robinson and Callighen. Even Park Superintendent George Bartlett dropped by the Lodge one evening to meet Tom Thomson's fellow artist friend from the city.

"Any friend of Tom's is welcome here," was the answer Jackson usually received whenever he mentioned Thomson's name. Wherever he went around Canoe Lake and the surrounding area, he heard stories about Tom Thomson the fisherman, Tom Thomson the expert canoe handler. The name, he said, was like a password in the tightly knit northern community. If you were friends with Tom, you must be okay.

At first, painting was impossible in the extreme cold. Jackson had heard from some older artists that oil paint becomes gummy and hard to spread when it reaches very cold temperatures. Sure enough, the bitter cold snap during his first few days at the lake rendered his paints useless. But once the weather improved, he was out on his snowshoes every day, making sketches for later canvases.

Tom would like to paint this, Jackson often thought as he came upon a striking stand of birch trees or an especially jagged shoreline. In doing so, he eventually realized that Thomson's intimate knowledge of the wilderness was influencing him every bit as much as his knowledge of Impressionism and formal painting techniques were influencing Thomson.

Thomson's work commitments and obsession with developing his painting technique kept him in Toronto for the duration of Jackson's stay in Algonquin Park. When Jackson returned to Toronto in the early spring, loaded down with dozens of fresh new sketches, he found that the student had made remarkable progress — and had even scored a major victory.

"Look at this," Thomson said, thrusting a letter at Jackson before he even had a chance to set down his heavy bags. It was from the Ontario Society of Artists, informing Thomson that *Moonlight, Early Evening* — that canvas Jackson had helped him paint with van Gogh-like dashes of bright yellows — had been bought by the National Gallery!

As the artists and their friends celebrated the big sale that evening, someone pointed out that this was in fact the second

Thomson work to be bought for a big government collection — not bad for someone who had been painting for less than two years.

Thomson's ruddy face was flush with the heady success, but deep down he was terrified. Sooner or later, he realized, he would be exposed as a fraud. He could keep up the confident façade, but with all these new ideas swimming around in his head, he had to admit that he really didn't know what he was doing.

I never should have listened to that Jackson! he thought. *I never should have accepted Dr. MacCallum's support! I'm going to make a damn fool of myself!*

But now that he had fully committed himself, he knew he had no choice but to forge ahead. His fishing tackle came down off the wall and was packed up along with a supply of blank wooden panels and his oil paints, and he got ready to catch the next train north to Algonquin Park.

This familiar image of Tom Thomson in his canoe, fixing a fly or lure, was taken by Maud Varley in Algonquin Park in the autumn of 1914.

6

Bursts of Light and Colour

Dr. MacCallum's summer cottage on Go Home Bay was as rustic as its surroundings. Set amidst white rocks and weathered old pine trees, it offered a panoramic view of a picturesque corner of Georgian Bay. From the ever-changing skies overhead to the choppy blue-green water, there was a lot of material for the landscape painter and it was quickly becoming a popular sketching ground for Dr. MacCallum's Toronto artist friends.

Jackson, Lismer, and MacDonald had all spent time there, and in the early summer of 1914 it was Thomson's turn.

After spending the late winter sketching in a snowy Algonquin Park, Thomson had spent most of May camping and sketching with Lismer at Smoke Lake. He then paddled and portaged his way to Parry Sound, where he met Dr. MacCallum. A few days later they were down at the cottage. Thomson settled in for a summer of sketching and fishing among the surrounding islands. It was here that he gathered material for his large canvas, *Pine Island, Georgian Bay* — a composition of two large pines blown by an early evening wind.

But even at remote Go Home Bay, the problems of the outside world were never far away.

Newspapers were brought in regularly on a supply boat that served the cottage community, and each evening Thomson and Dr. MacCallum would sit by the big stone fireplace reading about the growing trouble on the other side of the ocean.

"They say Europe is being described as a political powder keg about to blow up," Dr. MacCallum said gravely as he read the latest news. "It says here that things have been getting worse over there for the past forty years. Now they're very worried."

Then it happened.

On June 28, the heir to the Austrian throne, Archduke Franz Ferdinand, was shot and killed by a Serbian assassin while visiting Sarajevo. This set off a month-long chain of events that exploded into a declaration of war by the first week of August. The Allied nations of Great Britain, France, and Russia were lined up against the Axis powers of Germany, Austria-Hungary, and the Ottoman Empire. Although the United States declared itself neutral, Canada immediately rallied behind Great Britain and its allies. Within days, the call for recruits went out as young men were hastily trained for combat and sent overseas.

Thomson's first reaction to the news was that he should head back to Toronto and present himself at a recruiting office.

"Don't bother," Dr. MacCallum said. "They say the war won't last past Christmas. You'd only be halfway across the ocean and would have to turn back."

That settled the matter between them — or so they both thought.

* * *

Always the guiding influence, Dr. MacCallum kept encouraging Thomson to paint. He kept in touch with Jackson, who was out west sketching the Rockies and would head straight to Algonquin Park upon his return so that he and Thomson could sketch the blazing autumn foliage. At the same time, Lismer got in touch with them to announce his plans to return to the park in the fall, and Thomson invited Fred Varley to join them. Through a series of letters sent back and forth across the country, it was arranged that Thomson would host a major sketching party in October — and at the same time he would again be exposed to the techniques of seasoned landscape artists. Thomson was thrilled at the prospect and, as Jackson would describe it, began "stirring up his red paint for the fray."

The leaves at Go Home Bay had not yet started to change colour when Thomson loaded up his canoe with food and camping gear and said goodbye to the MacCallum family. It was a good time to leave, he wrote to MacDonald, because between the MacCallums and their various guests, neighbours, and social activities, Go Home Bay was beginning to feel too much like Rosedale. He needed solitude after being around so many people, so he planned to paddle all the way to Algonquin Park by himself. There was no direct water route; his only choice was to head north on Georgian Bay, past Parry Sound, to the mouth of the French River. Then he would paddle east to Lake Nipissing and follow the South River down into Algonquin Park — a trip of more than two hundred kilometres.

Sure enough, it was a gruelling — but glorious — journey. There were a few short portages along the way, but Thomson was strong and managed to carry everything between the waterways whenever necessary, even if it took him two trips. He camped in sheltered spots, catching fish for supper, and set off again early each morning. Throughout it all he watched what he had heard Dr. MacCallum call the pageant of the north — the gradual turning of the maple and birch leaves to red and yellow, then the slow shift from green to gold of the scraggly tamaracks.

Within a week he was back in familiar territory. His canoe appeared from around the bend at Canoe Lake and pulled up at the Mowat Lodge dock. His Algonquin Park friends were all there to greet him — Shannon Fraser, Mark Robinson, Larry Dickson, and all the other regulars. Thomson had only been coming to the park for two years now, but he was already somewhat of an institution around Canoe Lake. Never mind the melting snow or darkening ice — Tom Thomson's arrival at Algonquin Park signalled the official start of spring. Now, whenever he stepped off the train at Canoe Lake Station or paddled his canoe up to Mowat Lodge, he was home.

In September, Alex Jackson blew into Algonquin Park like a late summer storm, joking with the conductor in his loud, booming voice as he swung his two big knapsacks off the baggage car. Thomson and Fraser were both waiting to meet him at the station, and they drove him back to Mowat Lodge on Fraser's horse-drawn wagon.

"It's good to be back in familiar territory," Jackson said as he gazed out over Canoe Lake. He had spent the past five months in the Rockies, sketching the mountains in remote railway construction camps. He was tired of painting only grey, vertical rocks and green fir trees. The reds and yellows of the turning maples and birches caught his eye right away, and he was already spotting flashes of violet and orange in the underbrush before they reached the lodge.

For the first few days of their sketching trip, Thomson and Jackson loaded up the canoe and headed south to Tea Lake, where they devoted themselves to capturing the autumn colours. Jackson was always ready with some helpful advice whenever Thomson got stuck on a sketch, patiently showing him how to re-arrange the composition or add a complementary colour to brighten up the foliage. But while Thomson was the student when it came to painting, the roles were suddenly reversed when it came to camping, fishing, and handling the canoe. This was when Thomson became the teacher, showing Jackson everything from how to build up a roaring campfire in just a few minutes to how to land a speckled trout before it wriggled off the hook.

As Jackson quickly learned, anyone camping in the wilderness with Thomson was sure to eat well. There was always a large knapsack stashed in the bottom of his canoe filled with bacon, beans, flour, eggs, and coffee. His specialty was bannock, a flatbread that he fried on a hot stone. It was from an ancient Scottish recipe handed down from his grandmother Betty, which he adapted for the campfire from a similar Native recipe. This always went well with the daily supply of trout he caught, then baked in a small, portable camp oven.

Jackson observed Thomson carefully, picking up camping and canoeing skills that would serve him well for the rest of his life.

Travelling slowly along the shoreline, Thomson paddled the canoe while Jackson kept a sharp lookout for interesting subjects to sketch. There were beaver dams, arrangements of driftwood, dead grey spruce trees, dark pines standing out against a bright yellow background of birches, not to mention an ever-changing sky overhead.

Whenever they stopped to sketch, Thomson would attack his panel vigorously, laying on the paint in thick strokes. Dark blue water, white clouds, orange hillsides — everything was rendered quickly and spontaneously, as if Thomson was eager to capture that very moment in time. Jackson was impressed by his friend's progress since they last worked together, in the Studio Building the previous winter.

"Tom is doing some exciting stuff," Jackson wrote to Dr. MacCallum. "He keeps one up to time. Very often I have to figure out if I am leading or following. He plasters on the paint and gets fine quality — but there is a danger in wandering too far down that road."

Sometimes Jackson had to restrain Thomson from imitating his style. The outstanding quality of Thomson's work was its raw energy and honest depiction of the landscape, while Jackson took a more poetic approach. If Thomson tried to paint like Jackson, his sketch somehow lost its impact.

"Dr. MacCallum told me the same thing," Thomson admitted. "He said, 'Don't follow that Jackson too closely — paint in your own style.'"

Still, finding his own unique style was often difficult for Thomson. One evening, while sketching a sunset on Smoke Lake, he found that he couldn't get the right effect of the light reflecting on the water. One way looked too much like Jackson's style, so he scraped off the paint and tried again. That didn't look right either, so out came the knife again and he scraped the panel down to the wood.

Later, while he stared at the finished sketch by the light of the campfire, it looked worse yet. He grabbed the sketch in frustration and threw it into the darkness. Then, in a sudden rage, he stood up and threw his sketch box far into the bush.

"I'm through!" he shouted at Jackson. "I always said I'd make a damn fool of myself, and I was right! I can't even paint a simple damned sunset! I can't paint like you or Harris or any of the others! I quit!"

Knowing his friend's sudden mood swings, Jackson said nothing. He simply watched as Thomson stormed down to where his canoe was tied and angrily paddled off into the night. An hour passed and he had not returned, but Jackson was not worried. He knew that Thomson often spent the whole night in his canoe, crawling beneath the thwarts and sleeping comfortably as he slowly drifted out in the middle of a lake — under the stars and away from the mosquitoes.

Jackson crawled into the tent and went to sleep. Early the next morning, he was awakened by the clatter of frying pans and the smell of coffee and bacon. Outside the tent, he could hear Thomson whistling away to himself.

"Wake up, Alex!" Thomson shouted cheerfully. "You have to help me find my sketch box. There's a big beaver dam down by the end of the lake. I don't think we've sketched there yet!"

After a hearty breakfast, they crawled through the bushes, picking up paint tubes and panels. They found Thomson's broken sketch box and took it to the Smoke Lake ranger, Bud Callighen, to repair it.

Then they set off down the lake to find that beaver dam.

The autumn colours grew in brilliance as the season progressed. Dr. MacCallum's annual "pageant of the north" was reaching its climax just as Arthur Lismer, Fred Varley, and their wives were met at the Canoe Lake station by Fraser's wagon. The tamaracks had turned to a warm, bright gold, and the birch leaves were

Photo by Maud Varley

Always eager to show off his beloved Algonquin Park, Tom Thomson hosted his Toronto artist friends at Canoe Lake in the fall of 1914. In the rear, from left, are Thomson, A.Y. Jackson, and Arthur Lismer; in front are Fred Varley, baby Marjorie Lismer, and her mother, Esther.

reaching an exciting shade of pale yellow. Now the ground was covered in yellow and orange leaves as well, giving the entire landscape a higher, lighter tone. This was contrasted by the lakes, which grew colder and turned dark blue.

Thomson and Jackson welcomed their friends with a picnic out behind Mowat Lodge, where the Lismers and Varleys had booked rooms. Maud Varley took a photograph of the party, including Esther Lismer and baby daughter Marjorie. Afterwards, as Thomson and Lismer went off to forage for some firewood, Lismer took him aside. "I have a message for you from Dr. MacCallum," he said in his strong Yorkshire accent.

Thomson was stung, for he immediately knew what was coming. He felt his anger growing as he shot back, "Yes, and I'll bet I know what it is! He said, 'Don't let that Jackson fellow influence him too much!'"

A startled Lismer nodded as Thomson threw down an armful of firewood and marched off into the woods. He lit his pipe and spent a few minutes trying to cool off in the shade of some black spruces. *I don't need anyone telling me not to copy Jackson!* he thought. *I'll have a style of my own yet!*

With that, he resolved to paint his own way — never mind what Dr. MacCallum or any of the others might think! Starting the next day, when he led his three friends on their next sketching expedition in the park, he wouldn't allow himself to be influenced by how they painted.

"I know the perfect place to start," Thomson said brightly as his three friends prepared their boxes for a day's sketching. Soon they were following him through the colourful woods to the guide Larry Dickson's place. Earlier that year, while the snow was still thick on the ground, Thomson had sketched Dickson's shack — a low, crudely built cabin with a huge tree stump at the front entrance, set among a thick grove of birch trees. Dickson welcomed the artists to his home, but he had to admit that he was puzzled by their interest in his little shack.

Thomson and Lismer both got busy with their sketch boxes, but the resulting images were quite different. Thomson painted the shack amidst bare birch trunks, with gold tamaracks in the background, while Lismer painted the trees fully decked out in yellow and gold leaves. This, as Thomson learned that night as the artists huddled around the campfire discussing the day's work, was Lismer's way of using the Impressionist technique of placing complementary colours next to each other.

"Monet does that all the time," Jackson said. "I saw a lot of his canvases in France where he used complementary colours to brighten up his subjects."

In Lismer's sketch, which he would later call *The Guide's Home*, the yellow and orange birch leaves against the blue sky created a visually vibrant effect that he would later develop fully when he painted a very successful canvas from that sketch.

The landscape was so inspiring that even Varley, first and foremost a portrait artist, found much to paint in the tangled brush and boulders set against the backdrop of an endless forest. He sketched many images of Maud posed amidst the Algonquin Park landscape, and even made some studies of lakes and hills. Thomson's enthusiasm had awakened his dormant appreciation for landscape painting. "The country is a revelation to me, and completely bowled me over at first," Varley wrote to Dr. MacCallum that week from Mowat Lodge.

"Varley, Lismer and company are enjoying themselves thoroughly. Out all the time," Jackson confirmed in his next letter to Dr. MacCallum. "And the weather has been glorious. In fact they have had as much good weather in the last twelve days as Tom and I have had in a month."

This was certainly true. In all, the 1914 autumn sketching trip in Algonquin Park was memorable for all four artists. The bursts of light and colour in the trees, on the hills, and reflected in the water inspired them to produce what would later become some of their most successful canvases. But it was not all happiness and laughter, as the war in Europe cast a constant pall over their conversations. Any time they happened to see a newspaper, the front pages were invariably filled with grim news from the front lines. Casualty lists were published regularly, and one fact was tragically obvious to everyone — Canadian boys were dying at an alarming rate.

* * *

Back in Toronto in the middle of November, Thomson arrived at the Studio Building to find Jackson working on a large canvas of the sketch he had painted below Tea Lake Dam a month earlier. "I'll probably call it *The Red Maple*," Jackson said as Thomson watched him lay in bright shades of scarlet and crimson to depict the leaves of a maple sapling in front of the dark blues and foamy whites of the rushing Ox Tongue River.

"I'm going back to Montreal," Jackson said. "This war is bothering me too much. I think I'll go down and see a few people, then join up and see if I can't do my part."

He went on to tell Thomson that when he had told Harris of his plans, Harris offered to use his family connections to secure him an officer's commission. "But I told him no, I don't know anything about the military, so I had better start off at the bottom, as a private, like everyone else."

Jackson completed *The Red Maple* and left the wet canvas with MacDonald, asking him to make sure it was entered in the Ontario Society of Artists' spring exhibition. Within two weeks, he was back in Montreal.

The damned war!

Thomson was horrified by what the war had done to the city in just a few months. From the recruiting posters in store windows to the legions of young men marching in formation on their way to the train station, Toronto was completely different from the city he had left in early April.

One afternoon, shortly after his return from Algonquin Park, Thomson was standing at the corner of Yonge and Bloor streets with Fred and Maud Varley, watching row upon row of new recruits march past. Thousands of men and boys, marching eight abreast, passed them in just a few minutes. It was a sight that inspired patriotism in many of those watching on the sidewalk, but this quickly turned to despair when they realized that many of these young men would never return.

"Gun fodder for a day," Thomson observed bitterly. "They're marching to their deaths."

"They say it won't last very long at all," Varley said, trying to sound as optimistic as possible. "Six months at the most. The boys should be home for Christmas."

"Six months, hell!" Thomson cried. "Three or four years it must be!"

7

In the Northland

Fred Varley was wrong about the war not lasting very long. As 1914 turned to 1915, the daily newspaper reports from Europe showed no signs of an end to the carnage. Lists of casualties were regularly posted in the local papers, bringing the tragedy painfully close to home.

Filled with anger and disgust, Thomson presented himself at a Toronto recruiting office and asked to enlist in the infantry. He knew Dr. MacCallum would object, but this was much more important than painting. There would be plenty of time to paint after the Germans were beaten.

"Sorry, you've been rejected," he was told by a young sergeant after spending most of the afternoon waiting in long lines and taking a physical examination that could not have lasted more than thirty seconds.

Again, "weak lungs" was the official reason he was given when he asked why he could not serve.

Thomson prepared to face a long winter in Toronto. He knew the next few months would not be easy, for Dr. MacCallum's year of financial support had now expired. He would have to be frugal, saving his pennies and skipping meals until most of the snow melted and he could get back up to Algonquin Park.

With Jackson gone and commercial art jobs made scarce by the war, Thomson could not afford to pay Harris the twenty-two dollars monthly rent for Studio One by himself. Luckily, Frank Carmichael, his friend from Grip, was also looking for studio space and he agreed to split the rent with Thomson.

A native of Orillia, Ontario, twenty-four-year-old Carmichael was a quiet, bespectacled commercial artist who, like Jackson, had formally studied art in Europe before the war — in fact his recent studies in Antwerp had been cut short by the hostilities, forcing him to return to Canada. He shared a passion for landscape painting with his Toronto colleagues and loved nothing more than to spend a weekend afternoon on the outskirts of the city, sketching in watercolour.

Carmichael and Thomson got on well together, both as studio mates and as fellow artists, despite the thirteen-year difference in their ages. Just as he had done with Jackson, Thomson paid close attention to Carmichael's European technique as he painted, picking up valuable tips on composition and how to render certain effects of light on the canvas — but this time he was determined to paint in his own distinct style.

The trouble was finding a subject that would allow him to express himself the way he wanted. He searched through his

Algonquin Park sketches, but nothing stirred his imagination. Then he found it — a small sketch of dead spruce trees by a riverbank he had completed the previous year in his studio. This sketch, which he had painted in water-based gouache rather than oil, reminded him of a Scandinavian painting he had once seen, where the branches of dead fir trees formed a decorative screen between the viewer and the river beyond.

He rolled up his sleeves and stretched a large canvas. After priming it with a cream-coloured base, he used a large brush to fill the foreground with a careful arrangement of black, dark blue, and brown spruce trunks. The composition had to be just right, with a thick cluster of trees on the right balanced by a larger tree on the left, the two sides connected by a central tree leaning between them. Then he used a much thinner brush to add an intricate network of branches. In doing so he was combining his training in commercial design with his keen observations of the deep woods. He had to be careful not to have too many trees and dead branches in the foreground, as that would obliterate the background. But at the same time he had to have enough to suggest a tangled jungle of spruces. Only after he finished all the trees did he start painting the sky and bright autumn foliage in the background, carefully adding the colours between the branches and tree trunks. In doing so he often left tiny traces of the cream-coloured canvas exposed between the branches, giving the whole painting a brighter atmosphere.

Once finished, Thomson lit his pipe and stood back from the canvas. *Yes, this is what I wanted to say*, he thought.

Today, Thomson's *Northern River* is famous for its honest portrayal of the Canadian wilderness. But, in 1915 it was a bold statement — so bold that when the Ontario Society of Artists held its annual spring exhibition, Thomson packed up *Northern*

River and submitted it to the panel. It was accepted, along with Jackson's *Red Maple* and Lismer's Impressionist-inspired canvas of Larry Dickson's shack, *The Guide's Home.*

"Well, you three fellows have outdone yourselves this year," a delighted MacDonald wrote to Thomson in Algonquin Park a few weeks later. "The National Gallery has bought *The Guide's Home, The Red Maple,* and *Northern River!*"

Thomson was overjoyed by the news, for he certainly needed the five hundred dollars, but the first thing he did was head over to Larry Dickson's place to inform him that Lismer's painting of his little shack was now hanging in Ottawa.

"I sure hope he got a fair price for it," Dickson said.

When Thomson told him just how much it had been worth, Dickson's jaw dropped and he gasped. "This whole place ain't worth half as much!"

Thomson returned to Toronto in the late fall of 1915 to find the newspapers still filled with grim news of the war overseas. Things were only getting worse. More than a year had now passed, and there was no end in sight.

Jackson had enlisted in the 60th Infantry Battalion in Montreal and was now in England, training for trench warfare in the front lines of France or Belgium.

"I can't get used to Jackson being in the machine," Thomson had written to MacDonald from Algonquin Park that summer, "and it is rotten that in this so called civilized age that such things can exist but since this war has started it will have to go on until one side wins out and of course there is no doubt which side it will be, and we will see Jackson back on the job once more."

Thomson had been uncannily accurate in referring to the war as a machine. To him, it was a huge, unstoppable force that rolled over every aspect of life and destroyed everything in its path. Everywhere he looked in Toronto there were recruiting posters calling for all able-bodied men to answer the call to fight. Yonge Street windows displayed caricatures of the evil Kaiser Wilhelm and the noble John Bull, while carefully worded slogans played on young men's consciences: "Get into a real man's uniform," said one. "You said you would go when you were needed ... You are needed NOW!"

These recruiting posters had been very effective, Thomson noticed, for he saw countless young men in uniform — and worse, young men with missing limbs. The sight of it made him sick. Filled with outrage, he again marched into the nearest recruiting office and filled out the paperwork. He submitted to a physical examination — but again he was turned away.

Thomson's temper rose, but he calmly put on his coat and hat and left the recruiting office, muttering to himself. How could a man who could carry a canoe and all his camping gear over a rough portage possibly suffer from weak lungs? He immediately resolved to try his luck at another recruiting office — hopefully one whose doctor had a faulty stethoscope — but that plan was quickly scuttled.

"What's this I hear of you trying to join the war?" a gruff Dr. MacCallum asked when he caught wind of his intentions.

"I've been staring at those recruiting posters so long, I'm beginning to believe them," Thomson replied. "I want to do my part."

"You have no business running off to the army!"

"Jackson's already over there and Harris is waiting for his officer's commission ..."

"You can better serve your country as an artist, not a soldier!"

This made no sense to Thomson, but he had always respected Dr. MacCallum and trusted his judgment. He knew he could never enlist, strongly suspecting that Dr. MacCallum had spread the word among his professional colleagues in all the local recruiting offices to reject Thomson on any grounds, from "flat feet" to "weak lungs."

Their conversation ended any further question of Thomson going to war — but it did not solve a more immediate problem, for it looked like he might not even have a place to live in Toronto for the coming winter, not even on Severn Street.

Frank Carmichael had recently vacated the studio they had shared, leaving him with no one to split the expenses. Twenty-two dollars per month was a reasonable rent, but Thomson knew it was well beyond his meagre budget. Thanks to the war it was difficult to find commercial art jobs, and people were not exactly lining up to buy his sketches. Besides, all six units in the Studio Building had already been rented for the winter.

The problem was soon solved by Lawren Harris. Behind the Studio Building, about ten paces from the rear entrance, an old wooden shack stood against the steep slope of the ravine. Originally a cabinetmaker's workshop, it had been used most recently as a tool shed during construction of the Studio Building. Now it was abandoned and forgotten, and had fallen into a bad state of disrepair.

Thomson had had his eye on this modest little structure for a long time. It reminded him of a prospector's shack or a guide's home deep in the woods. It was damp and decrepit, with neither plumbing nor electricity, and it smelled badly of old wood and mildew. Still, it was certainly no worse than some of the places he had lived in up in the wilderness. He strolled out back one afternoon and inspected the shack, judged it to be more than adequate for his modest needs, then went back inside to see Harris.

"It certainly needs a lot of work, Tom," was Harris's immediate response. The request came as no surprise, for Harris had always sensed that his friend did not feel entirely at home in the city. "We could fix it up and you could spend your winters in that shack, living just as you would out in the bush — but you would still be five minutes from Yonge Street."

Harris, an ardent student of philosophy, immediately saw a strong similarity between Thomson and Henry David Thoreau, the nineteenth-century American philosopher whose writings about nature had had a profound influence on most of the Studio Building artists. Jim MacDonald had even named his son after Thoreau.

"That shack could be your version of Thoreau's cabin at Walden Pond," Harris said as he put on his overcoat and followed Thomson outside.

Thomson was familiar with Thoreau, especially the period he had spent living alone in a cabin he had built himself by the shore of a wilderness pond in Massachusetts. Thoreau's experiment in self-reliance was chronicled in his book *Walden*, or *Life in the Woods*, one of Thomson's favourite works of literature — right up there with *The Compleat Angler*. While he relished the idea of reliving Thoreau's experience, he was also looking forward to the solitude of the shack, where he could work alone and undisturbed on his canvases throughout the winter months.

"You'll need a big window here," Harris said, pointing to the east wall. "You'll also need heat."

"I'll be fine," Thomson insisted, already eager to move in.

The next day, Harris consulted Dr. MacCallum, who co-owned the property, and a work crew was summoned to Severn

Street. The soggy old floorboards were ripped up and a fresh new floor put down, the roof patched up, several rotting boards replaced, and an electric light installed. Within just a few days, and for less than two hundred dollars, the dark, damp, and droughty old shack was transformed into a bright, comfortable work space and living quarters. Thomson got busy himself, building a bunk bed, shelves, and a table, not to mention a sturdy easel that could accommodate large canvases. Before the first snowstorm hit the city, Thomson was living comfortably in the shack, his sketches and fishing tackle hung carefully on the walls, with coffee boiling and bacon sizzling on the woodstove.

Again, Harris and Dr. MacCallum had come to Thomson's rescue. They agreed to charge him only one dollar per month to live in the shack, leaving him free to spend most of his money on art supplies. The only thing he had to do, they told him, was keep painting.

News of Thomson's unique little *Walden*-in-Toronto winter home spread quickly. Soon the shack was a favourite destination for visitors, and he found himself playing the role of host more often than he had ever expected.

At first, the shack was such a novelty that it was customary for anyone visiting one of the Studio Building artists to go out back and knock on Thomson's door as well. These frequent interruptions made it difficult for him to paint. He often worked on several canvases at once, turning his attention from one to another as ideas came to him. This meant there was usually a large canvas on his easel, half-finished or barely started, and several more, in various stages of completion, leaning against the walls of the shack. They drew most visitors' attention, and Thomson had to be firm but polite in refusing to show them off. More than anything, he hated anyone seeing what he was

Photo courtesy Jennifer McKnight.

Tom Thomson's shack, which served as his rustic winter quarters in Toronto in 1915–16 and 1916–17. In 1962 it was moved from its spot behind the Studio Building and reassembled on the grounds of the McMichael Canadian Collection in Kleinburg, Ontario, where it still stands today.

working on. With the exceptions of Dr. MacCallum, Harris, Lismer, and MacDonald, no one was allowed to see any works-in-progress, so he often had to drop everything and scramble around to hide his unfinished canvases whenever he saw someone approaching the shack.

A frequent visitor to the shack was MacDonald's teenage son, Thoreau, a budding artist himself and keen naturalist. His account of the shack offers a clear image of how Thomson spent his winters in the city:

> He had a bunk and a little cast iron range for heat and cooking; the shack was clean and tidy. Sometimes he invited me to stay for meals and I remember well the woodsman's flourish with which he threw a handful of tea into the pot and mashed the potatoes with an empty bottle, adding what looked like half a pound of butter. While we ate he drummed his fingers on the table with great speed and vigour. I suppose he was anxious for me to go so that he could get to his work again.

Working at his big easel throughout the day left little time for Thomson to stay in shape. Up in the north country he spent most of his days paddling his canoe, chopping firewood, or carrying his gear through the woods. His diet was sparse, for he normally ate only what he could either catch or carry. As a result, he would return to Toronto in the late fall in top physical condition. But over the winter months, the only exercise he got was walking to a nearby store for supplies — or to one of his favourite restaurants.

He remedied this by exercising as much as possible. Lismer, who often shared studio space in the shack, loved to recall how Thomson took great pride in his own agility, and insisted on showing visitors a trick he had perfected. Lighting in the shack consisted of several bare bulbs suspended from the ceiling, each turned on or off by a long, thin chain that dangled within easy reach. "Watch this!" Thomson would say to any first-time visitor as he backed up, took a short run at the chain, leaped high in the air, and grabbed the chain between his feet. The light would snap on and Thomson would land squarely on the floor.

His major form of winter exercise consisted of strapping on his snowshoes each night and hiking the length of Rosedale Ravine, then out into the countryside well beyond Toronto city limits. The Studio Building artists soon grew accustomed to the silent, dark silhouette of their friend making his way in the moonlight. Sometimes he would not return to the shack until daybreak — exhausted but happy — ready to face another day of challenges at his easel.

Thanks to the shack, the woodsman could finally be comfortable in the city.

One of the first canvases Thomson painted in the shack was a bright autumn view of a wilderness hillside next to a lake, seen through a screen of white birch trees. Based on a sketch he had painted in Algonquin Park just two months earlier, the canvas would borrow the Impressionist technique of placing complementary colours next to each other to achieve added brilliance. He rendered the background lake a deep blue — the cold, dark blue that he only saw in the late fall — which helped the bright yellow and orange foliage of the birch forest stand out.

Then he added the painting's most striking feature — a fallen dead tree that lay horizontally across the composition, drawing the viewer's eye straight into the middle of the birch trees and the dark lake beyond.

This looks nothing like anything Jackson has ever done, Thomson thought with great satisfaction as he stepped back from his easel. *Or Lismer or MacDonald for that matter!* Yes, just as he had done with *Northern River* the previous winter, Thomson had rendered the autumn wilderness in a style that he knew was distinctly his own. This new canvas, which would eventually be titled *In the Northland*, was the next step forward.

In the early spring of 1916, Thomson appeared at the Trainor home in Huntsville, weighed down by camping gear and sketching materials. Hugh Trainor was a foreman with one of the lumber companies operating in Algonquin Park, and he and Thomson had grown quite friendly over the past three years — in fact Thomson was now close to the whole family, having spent many pleasant evenings on the dock of their summer cottage at Canoe Lake, just down from Mowat Lodge.

Now, whenever Thomson was heading to the park in the spring or returning to Toronto in the fall, he was expected to drop in on the Trainors at their large Huntsville home to enjoy two or three days of their hospitality. These stays had begun as casual visits, but after a couple of years they took on great importance, for Thomson felt himself growing closer and closer to the Trainors' eldest daughter, Winnifred. More than ten years had passed since Alice Lambert's shriek of mocking laughter drove Thomson from Seattle; now he sometimes thought he might be ready for a steady relationship again, and he noticed Winnie in a way he had never considered before. She was tall and slender with brown hair and high cheekbones, and he was very fond of her musical voice and gentle sighs.

"I don't much care for painting," Winnie said when he showed her a few of his sketches. "I don't see how anyone could enjoy fishing," she said when he proudly held up a shiny lure he had just fashioned from a few wires and a piece of metal. Thomson had to admit that he and Winnie Trainor had very little in common, but that did not matter to him. He loved the way she reached for his hand whenever they walked together. As much as he hated to admit it, for the first time in years, he was actually smitten.

Be careful — don't let this one get away, he told himself, much the way he would if a big trout had just taken his lure and was struggling to break free.

Then it happened. Just as Thomson was saying his goodbyes to Winnie's parents and gathering his gear for the next train to Canoe Lake, Winnie took him aside.

"When are you going to ask me to marry you, Tom?"

Thomson was trapped. His mind raced wildly, but the words would not come. "Any time now, Winnie," was all he could manage — then he realized the full impact of his words.

8

The Pageant of the North

The year 1916 began very well for Thomson, with more good news from the annual Ontario Society of Artists exhibition. This time around, the National Gallery bought *Spring Ice*, a canvas depicting the retreat of winter from a dark blue Canoe Lake, for three hundred dollars.

Thomson arrived in Algonquin Park with the money bulging from his pocket, but no sooner had he announced his good news the first night in Mowat Lodge than Shannon Fraser took him aside.

"It's swell that you got all that money, Tom," he said, lowering his voice. "I was hoping you might help me out. See, I need to replace a few canoes here at the lodge before the summer tourist season begins, and I'm a bit short of ready cash. Can you lend me a couple of hundred?"

"Gee, Shan, I was kind of hoping …"

"I really need those canoes, Tom."

Thomson sighed and relented. He took out his roll of money and counted two hundred dollars into Fraser's hand.

"I'll pay you back as soon as I can," Fraser said gratefully, pocketing the bills.

Thomson had not been back in Algonquin Park for more than a few weeks when he received three welcome guests — Lawren Harris, his cousin Chester Harris, and Dr. MacCallum. They had decided to take an extended holiday in the wilderness before Harris reported for military duty at Camp Borden, where had been commissioned as a musketry instructor.

The company was a blessing for Thomson, as it kept his mind off Winnie Trainor and the awkward predicament he had gotten himself into. Were they engaged? He was not sure — all he knew was that the Trainors would soon be arriving to open their lakefront cottage for the season, and Winnie would be expecting him to play the role of loving suitor. Or would she?

Harris had chosen a good time to visit, for the park was still in transition from winter to spring. The ice had broken up on the lakes, but there were snowdrifts lingering in sheltered spots and the nights were bone-chillingly cold. On their first night, sitting as close to Thomson's roaring campfire as they could, Harris and Dr. MacCallum relayed the latest news from Toronto. They said that the fighting in France and Belgium was raging on, and that the most recent letters from A.Y. Jackson reported that his infantry unit was moving up to the front lines.

But back home in Toronto, they said, poor Jim MacDonald had been fighting a bitter battle of his own after sending a few canvases to the Ontario Society of Artists' spring exhibition.

"Old Heck really had it in for our Jim," Harris said of *Saturday Night* magazine critic Hector Charlesworth, who reviewed the show. "He attacked *The Tangled Garden*, Jim's big garden piece, saying the subject was far too insignificant for a canvas that size …"

"And he had the audacity to suggest that *Rocks and Maple* and *The Elements* were so hideous that they should be re-titled *Hungarian Goulash* and *Drunkard's Stomach*," Dr. MacCallum continued.

"Now Jim has been branded in the press as the most radical artist in Toronto," Harris said with a chuckle. "He retaliated with a stinging rebuttal in the *Globe* — 'Bouquets From a Tangled Garden' they called it — where he gave Old Heck what for and pushed our agenda on Canadian art."

"The publicity is like gold," Dr. MacCallum added brightly.

But Thomson was not pleased. He felt his anger rising and quickly stood up.

"It's all very well and fine to be branded as a radical," he said, poking forcefully at the fire. "But don't forget, Jim has a family to support. This damned war has put a stop to a lot of commercial art commissions, and Jim is having a hard time of it. He can't sell many paintings as it is. He can't afford to be seen as second-rate or radical by the art-buying public. It's all fine for fellows like Alex Jackson to be branded a radical — he's a bachelor with no responsibilities, but MacDonald is the only breadwinner in his family. Damn that Charlesworth and his damned articles!"

With that, Thomson stormed off into the woods to cool off, leaving his friends by the campfire.

Always eager to play the role of wilderness guide, Thomson insisted that his friends join him on a trip up to the Cauchon Lake region, near the northern border of the park. They packed up two canoes with camping gear and set off on the gruelling sixty-kilometre trek, with Thomson leading them across lakes, through rapids, and on several exhausting portages through thick woods.

Still, the three visitors persevered and enjoyed the trip. They could not help but marvel at how Thomson seemed to know every bend in every river, and just where to stop for a portage. And when it came time to rest for the evening, Thomson had their tents up and a campfire blazing in the time it took Harris to prepare his sketch box. He was the ideal guide.

On the other hand, Thomson could not have hoped for a better sketching companion than Harris at this point in his development, for he was full of ideas and theories that had never occurred to Thomson. Harris was primarily concerned with expression — conveying a mood in his work — and their discussions inspired Thomson to see the landscape in a new way and seek out subjects he may not have considered before.

One of the first sketches Thomson completed during this trip came about one cold evening as the sun was setting on Little Cauchon Lake. He was immediately attracted to the forlorn shape of a huge pine tree standing alone on a plateau overlooking the lake. He painted its drooping boughs and bare, tendril-like branches as a silhouette against the yellow evening sky. The dark hills across the lake were bathed in deep shadows of blue and purple, and if he squinted hard enough, he could make out lingering traces of snow through the distant trees.

Later, Harris and Dr. MacCallum both praised the sketch as Thomson held it up in the light of the campfire. "You've captured the very essence of the north country on that panel," Dr. MacCallum said. "The loneliness, the weathered dignity ... You have said it all."

Inside, Thomson could not have been more pleased. But he was too modest to acknowledge the praise. "I suppose it's all right," he replied quietly, digging at the fire's embers with a stick.

Dr. MacCallum and Chester Harris had to return to Toronto after a few days, but the two artists continued working their way further south to Aura Lee Lake. It was here that Harris's encouragement to express emotion in his work got the better of Thomson — but resulted in another powerful sketch.

They were sketching in a clearing by the shore when the sky suddenly grew dark and distant rumblings grew louder. They sought shelter in an abandoned lumber shack nearby, and watched big grey clouds move swiftly over the lake.

Thomson had an idea. "I wonder if I can capture the fury of a thunderstorm as it happens," he said.

The wind picked up into a howling, invisible force that bent the tall spruce trees, and the first few raindrops spattered against the shack. But instead of staying inside, Thomson grabbed his sketch box and ran out into the rain. Harris watched in disbelief as he squatted next to a tree stump. He flipped open his sketch box and began mixing colours. Lightning flashed overhead and sent jagged forks into the choppy lake and into the hills on the far shore. With the thunder crashing all around him and the rain pelting the panel he was painting on, Thomson stood his ground against the spring storm, his wet black hair blown back by the wind. His brush darted back and forth across the panel, capturing the dark grey sky, the bent trees, and the turbulent whitecaps on the lake.

"He was one with the storm's fury, save that his activity, while keyed to a high pitch, was nonetheless controlled," was how Harris remembered the incident. "In twenty minutes, Tom had caught in living paint the power and drama of storms in the north."

But this was not the first time Thomson had thrown himself into the raging elements in order to get a good sketch: just a week earlier he had insisted on painting in a gale-force wind that was blowing in from the west and bending the lakeside pine trees at dangerously odd angles. He brought his sketch box close to one of the trees and began blocking out his composition on the panel. Before long, Harris and Dr. MacCallum watched in horror as the big tree's trunk suddenly snapped and Thomson disappeared into the chaotic shower of branches of massive pine boughs that came crashing down around him.

"The wind blew down the tree of the picture and Harris at first thought that Thomson was killed," Dr. MacCallum recalled. "But he soon sprang up, waved his hand to him and went on painting."

Both artist and sketch survived, and once finished, the sketch captured the very essence of a windy day on a northern lake. The swiftly moving overhead clouds and churning white-caps in the water, both rendered by just a few quick dashes of white, provided a dramatic backdrop for the big tree in the foreground — leaning precariously but still standing defiantly against the wind.

Harris packed up his gear and caught the train back to his summer home on Lake Simcoe, where he would prepare for his military service. Thomson could not face Winnie yet, so he went over to Cache Lake and dropped in on old George Bartlett, the park superintendent. He had always loved visiting Bartlett's office, as it was decorated as a shrine to the wilderness, with many stuffed and mounted animals on the walls and in display cases.

"Say, George, anything going in the way of fire ranger work?" he asked.

"You came at a very good time, Tom," said Bartlett, a big man with a drooping white moustache. "I need a few able-bodied men to follow some loggers working up in the eastern sector, around Achray."

"That's fine," Thomson replied quickly, having heard that fire rangers attached to logging operations usually had little to do except make sure the lumberjacks followed the park's fire regulations in their camps. Aside from that, they had their fishing lines in the water all day — and got paid for it! Between his rod and his sketch box, he was sure to have a good summer now.

A week later he reported for duty at the ranger's station on Grand Lake, not far from the Ottawa River, in a section that had been incorporated into Algonquin Park just two years earlier. He introduced himself to Ranger Ed Godin, who immediately pulled out a map and showed him the area they had been assigned to cover.

"From Grand Lake, here, we'll be following the Booth Lumber Company's log drive southeast down the Petawawa River," Godin said, running his finger along the river indicated on the map. "We follow them all the way to the eastern border of the park."

Godin's cabin, which he had named the Outside Inn, was the region's ranger headquarters. When Thomson heard the name, he laughed out loud. "That sure is a fine name for a place like this," he said. Later, when the ranger went off on an errand down the lake, Thomson found a plank of wood and took out his sketch box.

When Godin retuned that evening, he found a sign hanging above the front porch of his cabin — Out-Side-Inn — all smartly lettered by Thomson in what was probably his very last design job.

* * *

The summer of 1916 was especially dry, and the northern woods were in grave danger. Anything from an unattended campfire to a stray spark from the coal furnace of a passing locomotive could set off a disastrous forest fire.

There had been a few thunderstorms in the late spring — including the one Thomson had ran out into and sketched — but the sun shone down on Algonquin Park nearly every day throughout June and by early July the fire wardens were on high alert. Armed with axes, buckets, and shovels — their only weapons against a blaze — Thomson and Godin nervously reported for duty with the Booth Lumber Company's logging party on Grand Lake.

As it turned out, that sign above Godin's cabin porch was the most painting Thomson would manage for the next few weeks, as his duties as fire ranger took up much more time than he had expected. At any moment they expected to smell smoke or hear that dreaded cry of "Fire!"

"A dead spruce or pine can go up like that," Godin said, snapping his fingers. Thomson knew exactly what he meant, having tossed many a rust-coloured pine bough onto a campfire and seen it instantly erupt in a flash of crackling flames. As a result, Thomson and Godin had to watch the Booth lumbermen very closely as they drove logs down the lake and along the Petawawa River.

Part of the fire rangers' duties was to scout the surrounding area for tell-tale signs of fires. There were no fire towers in that new section of the park, so Thomson and Godin had to take turns climbing to the top of hills or scaling the tallest pine tree and scanning the green horizon with binoculars. Luckily, they did not see any smoke.

"We have had no fires so far," he wrote to MacDonald. "This is a great place for sketching. One branch of the river runs between walls of rock 300 feet straight up. Will camp here when this fire job is finished."

Finally, after a few rainy nights in August, the threat of forest fires had diminished and Thomson had more free time on his hands to sketch. He found that he could get some sketching in if he stationed himself near the door of the lumberjacks' cookhouse. There, with one eye on the cooking fire and one eye on his sketch box, he could complete two or three panels in a day. This was how he got the sketch for his later canvas *The Drive*, a sweeping composition of logs collected below the dam at Grand Lake.

For several more weeks Thomson and Godin followed the Booth men on their drive towards the Ottawa River to the east. When they got to the Petawawa Gorges, Thomson's sketch box came out again and he spent hours painting the dramatic early autumn scenery.

All in all, it was a good summer and Thomson was satisfied that he had accumulated enough good sketches to provide plenty of material for a productive winter at his easel in the shack.

Still, the war in Europe was never far from anyone's mind, even up in remote Algonquin Park.

Back at Canoe Lake in the autumn of 1916, Thomson was sitting with Winnie on the Trainor dock one afternoon when he happened to glance over at the Bletcher cottage, further down the lake. There was something odd about the scene — then he spotted it. Flying from the Bletchers' flagpole was not Canada's flag, the familiar Red Ensign. Instead, the American Stars and Stripes were flapping in the Canoe Lake breeze.

"That's not right," Thomson remarked. "They should be flying the Canadian flag."

"But the Bletchers are Americans," Winnie said. "They're from Buffalo."

"They're Germans. We are at war with Germany."

"What does it matter?" Winnie asked. "It's just a flag."

"It matters because they are Germans flying the flag of a country that is not even in the war," Thomson said. "Canadian men are being killed on the battlefields every day, while the Americans have shed no blood at all. It's insulting!"

"I'm sure they mean no harm," Winnie said, but Thomson shook his head.

"They might as well have a big portrait of Kaiser Wilhelm nailed up over their porch!"

Feeling his temper rising, Thomson quickly stood up and hurried away. The last thing he wanted to do was say something hurtful to Winnie.

Late that night a canoe pulled up silently at the Bletcher dock and a shadowy figure crept up to their flagpole. The next morning, Shannon Fraser noticed the Red Ensign that usually flew above Mowat Lodge was missing. But there, a few hundred metres down the shoreline, the Canadian flag could be seen snapping in the brisk autumn wind on the Bletcher family's flagpole.

Mr. and Mrs. Bletcher were mystified. Their American flag was nowhere to be found. Who could have done this to them? But their son, Martin Jr., knew exactly who to blame. This was not the first time that artist from Toronto had accused him of being a German sympathizer.

"I'll give him what he deserves," the younger Bletcher vowed.

Back in Toronto just as the first snow covered the ground, Thomson put in a supply of firewood and settled back into the shack with dozens of sketches to consider for large canvases. Many of the sketches had been painted while Thomson was following the loggers in Algonquin Park, and he decided that the first canvas to be stretched, primed, and placed upon his easel would be an homage to the lumberjacks he had befriended over the summer and fall.

One image that had particularly impressed him was the sight of three long, flat-bottom rowboats — known as pointers — towing a barge across a lake one fall afternoon. As he blocked in the composition he heard a knock at his door. It was Jim MacDonald, who was taking a break from his own work and thought he might drop in for a cup of tea. Naturally, the conversation turned to MacDonald's public fight with the critic Hector Charlesworth the previous spring.

"It really confounds me how some people seem so reluctant to accept new ideas in painting," MacDonald said in his usual quiet manner. "I realize that any publicity is in fact good publicity, but must they be so insulting?"

"It's just their way," Thomson replied. Already a few radical ideas of his own were racing through his mind. *If they want a fight,* he thought, *I'll give them something that will really upset them!*

The next day, MacDonald and Dr. MacCallum dropped by the shack to find Thomson hard at work on his new canvas. It was still rough, but they could see three long red rowboats, with lumberjacks at the oars, towing a flat barge carrying a group of men and a team of sturdy workhorses. Thomson was busily dabbing broad, horizontal strokes of pure red into the sky and water, and vertical strokes into the bulky hill in the background. Neither MacDonald nor MacCallum could recall ever seeing so much red in one painting. They looked at each other and shrugged, not sure how to react.

"This one is for Charlesworth!" Thomson said mischievously, spotting his guests' puzzled expressions.

"Another pageant of the north," Dr. MacCallum mused.

And what a pageant the finished product turned out to be. Finally titled *The Pointers*, Thomson's new canvas threw an entire palette's worth of colours at the viewer, with quick dabs of various shades of blues and greens competing for space with the bold reds in the sky, water, and background hill. It was sure to upset even the most open-minded critic — and when it came to the modern style of landscape art being produced in the Studio Building, Hector Charlesworth and many of his fellow critics were anything but open-minded.

The next canvas to be stretched, primed and placed on Thomson's easel would have a much different flavour, he decided. He had always liked the way his sketches showed traces of the reddish wooden panel between the brushstrokes, and was eager to reproduce that effect on canvas. So before he started, he mixed and brushed a thin coat of dark orange over the entire surface to give it the appearance of a blank panel. Once that was dry, he dug into his darkest greens and browns and blocked in the curving, drooping shape of the pine tree he had sketched during that memorable trip with Harris to Cauchon Lake the previous spring.

Dr. MacCallum had praised the sketch, calling it a true vision of the north, so now Thomson would create a much larger version, something that would say the same thing — but in a much louder voice.

As he worked, he decided to make a few changes to the sky and lake in the background. Recalling Harris's favourite method of rendering the sky as a series of short, even brushstrokes, he mixed several shades of yellow and light green and began laying in a brick-like pattern of horizontal strokes to express the early evening sky. As in *Northern River* and many of his other larger works, the canvas showed through between the brushstrokes, only this time the reddish-orange undercoat made everything seem to glow. From the sky and water to the dangling tendrils of the big tree, everything was tied together through brilliant orange outlines — the clever technique of an experienced designer.

Tom Thomson's work was prominently displayed in the Canadian section of the huge British Empire Exhibition at Wembley, England, in 1924. Seen here are his three best-known canvases — from left, The West Wind, Northern River, and The Jack Pine — along with a selection of his Algonquin Park sketches immediately below.

The Jack Pine, as this canvas would later be titled, was Thomson's greatest achievement. It would eventually become the most familiar painting in Canada, and — just as Dr. MacCallum had predicted when he saw the original sketch — stand as a symbol of the rugged young country itself. He wanted to show it off to everyone, but many of his closest friends were away because of the war.

With his confidence soaring, Thomson quickly started another canvas. This one would be a similar composition of a pine tree overlooking a lake, only now he would paint up the sketch he had been working on when the big pine was blown down around him during that spring gale at Cauchon Lake.

He began in a fury of enthusiasm, painting the wind-blown clouds and waves, but a problem soon arose. The sky and water were rendered realistically, for this was the only way Thomson could properly convey the blowing clouds and the churning, white-capped water of the lake. But the tree itself was highly stylized, much like *The Jack Pine* — only for that canvas everything was painted in the same style, so it had worked. *The West Wind* was not coming so easily. Thomson was torn between painting it realistically and creating a modern, highly stylized version of the original sketch. He knew he had to choose one or the other, but he could never decide.

In the end, he left unfinished canvas on his easel. He would think about it over the rest of the year and return to it when he got back from Algonquin Park next November.

Thomson arrived at Canoe Lake in early April 1917 with a strong sense of purpose. He had recently struck upon the idea of painting the changing season at Canoe Lake in a series of sketches, from late winter to summer. He would produce at least one sketch per day, capturing the melting black ice on the lakes and lingering traces of blue snow in the deepest shadows to the fully bloomed green foliage and blue water of late June.

With Mowat Lodge as his base, he faithfully went out every day and painted a sketch. Before long they had accumulated to the point where storage was becoming a problem.

"Say Mark, do you mind if I keep these sketches here in your cabin to dry?" he asked Robinson one day.

The ranger looked over some of the panels and whistled in amazement. Here was the changing season at Canoe Lake, day by day, in a series of colourful sketches rendered in his friend's distinctive style.

"I'm not sure I want to be responsible for these," Robinson replied, but Thomson was adamant.

"They won't take up much room, and they'll brighten up your place for awhile."

As soon as Robinson nodded, Thomson brought in several dozen panels and propped them up on any available surface inside the cabin.

The sketching was going very well, but it served only as a temporary diversion from Thomson's inner turmoil, for he was still haunted by his commitment to Winnie. It had now been a year since their unofficial engagement, and he knew she would soon be pressing him to get married. The last thing he wanted was to hurt her or lose the friendship of her family. But marriage would mean giving up his current lifestyle and possibly giving up painting altogether — something he could not do, especially now that he had found his own creative voice and was making excellent progress.

Hoping to put off the inevitable as long as possible, Thomson went to George Bartlett's office and bought a guide's licence. Then he wrote to Dr. MacCallum, inviting him to Algonquin Park for a fishing trip.

But no matter what he did, deep down he knew he could not keep running from Winnie forever.

9

An Overturned Canoe

From the hooks and lures hanging on his wall to the well-thumbed copy of *The Compleat Angler* he often carried with him, fishing was Tom Thomson's lifelong passion — and it is somehow fitting that fishing should figure prominently in his death.

Not long after completing his series sketches showing the change of season from winter to summer, Thomson did a lot of fishing during the first week of July. One of his favourite spots was a deep pool in the river just below the Joe Lake Dam, not far from Mowat Lodge.

One day, while Thomson and the ranger Mark Robinson were fishing in that pool, they spotted a big old speckled trout lurking in the rocks at the bottom.

"Must be a five-pounder," Robinson said, leaning over and squinting down into the murky water where the dark shape darted back and forth among the shadows.

"I'd say closer to eight pounds," Thomson replied.

"There's only one way to find out," Robinson said, and the two shook hands on the bet. The big fish suddenly had two lures jiggling and flashing in front of it, but it simply turned and swam off. For the next two hours they tried to catch it, but nothing seemed to attract its attention.

"Maybe he's blind," Robinson mused.

"No, that old fellow's an artist," Thomson replied. "He knows the real from the unreal. You can't fool him."

That night, Thomson went through his tackle and made himself a new lure, one that was sure to do the trick. He and Robinson returned with their fishing poles the next day, and the day after, but try as they might, they could not persuade the big trout to strike at their lures.

The week passed, and the fish remained at the bottom of the river below Joe Lake Dam.

Finally, on the morning of Sunday, July 8, Thomson complained to Shannon Fraser that none of his best lures had worked on the crafty old trout. "If I didn't know better, I'd swear that big fellow knows we're trying to catch it and is playing us for fools!"

"Let's go have a look," Fraser said, and the two grabbed their fishing gear and set off on the road toward Joe Lake Dam. Sure enough, the old trout was there — but he would have nothing to do with their lures.

The men fished in silence, but there was something on Thomson's mind. "Say, Shan," he said eventually, as it took him awhile to find the right words. "I hate to bring it up, but I was wondering if you might have some of that money I lent you last year … I really need to buy a new suit."

"Well, Tom, sure, but business at the Lodge is slow right

now and I'll need a week or two to raise it ... Why do you need a new suit?"

"Winnie."

A few minutes passed. Neither said a word until Thomson broke the awkward silence. "I have an idea," he said, reeling in his line. "I know where I can catch a few big ones down by Tea Lake

Fishing was Thomson's lifelong passion, and he took great pride in displaying his catch. Here he sits on the front steps of Mowat Lodge with its proprietor, Shannon Fraser (left) and Charles Robinson (right) in the spring of 1917, shortly before his death.

Dam. I'll paddle down there this afternoon, catch a big one, and tonight I'll leave it on Robinson's doorstep with a note. He's sure to think I finally caught this old fellow."

The men chuckled over the practical joke as they returned to Mowat Lodge. Thomson wasted no time in stashing his fishing gear in his canoe, grabbing a few supplies, and shoving off from Fraser's dock. "I'll be back in a few hours," he called out with a wave of his hand.

It was shortly before noon. A light drizzle had begun, and a few friends from the lodge gathered on the dock to wave at Thomson as he swiftly paddled off across the grey water. They laughed as Fraser told them about Thomson's joke. Soon, the lone figure in the canoe disappeared behind a screen of trees on a nearby island.

It was the last time he was seen alive.

Where's Tom? The question was on the lips of everyone around Mowat Lodge the next day when he had not returned from his fishing trip.

"I saw his canoe yesterday," Martin Bletcher Jr. said when Fraser asked if he had seen Thomson. "It was empty, drifting by itself."

Alarmed, Fraser asked why he hadn't reported it at once. Bletcher simply shrugged. He was known to hate Thomson and could not be expected to be very helpful. Fraser immediately went out and found the canoe, not far from where Bletcher had seen it. It was not only empty, but drifting upside down. It was obvious that something terrible had happened.

"He couldn't have drowned," Fraser told everyone hopefully. "He was a strong swimmer, and he could handle a canoe like no one I've ever known." But even he had to admit the empty canoe was an ominous sign.

An intensive search was organized. The Bletchers, the Trainors, all the park rangers, and most of the other summer cottagers along Canoe Lake quickly mobilized to scour the woods and shorelines, all calling out Thomson's name at regular intervals.

No response.

Many suggested that Thomson had simply decided to go off alone on a prolonged sketching trip in the woods, just as he had done so many times in the past. His canoe probably got loose, drifted away, and overturned in the wind. But as time went by, that slim possibility grew even less likely. Hope diminished each time someone shouted Thomson's name, only to be answered by an echo from across the solemn lake.

Ranger Mark Robinson, recently returned to Canoe Lake after being slightly wounded in action overseas, paddled along the shoreline, blowing his army-issued Vimy whistle and listening for the slightest answer from Thomson. All he heard in response were the shrieks of blue jays in the woods and hoots from loons on the water.

Finally, Fraser sent a telegram to the Thomson family in Owen Sound, informing them of their missing son. The next day, George Thomson arrived at the lake to help search for his younger brother — but by now no one was holding out any hope.

Meanwhile, Thomson's Toronto friends read the grim news in the July 13 *Globe*:

TORONTO ARTIST MISSING IN NORTH

Toronto art circles were shocked yesterday at the news received from Algonquin Park that

Tom Thomson, one of the most talented of the younger artists in the city, had been missing since Sunday and was thought to have been drowned or the victim of foul play. Mr. Thomson was last seen at Canoe Lake at noon on Sunday, and at 3.30 in the afternoon his canoe was found adrift in the lake, upside down. There was no storm, only a light wind prevailing, and the fact that both paddles were in place in the canoe as if for a portage, adds to the mystery. Mr. Thomson carried a light fishing rod and this and his dunnage bag were missing … There is still a chance that Mr. Thomson may be alive, but this is considered doubtful as four days' search has failed to find a trace of him.

"There is nothing more I can do here," George Thomson announced, rubbing the sweat from his bald head as he arrived back at Mowat Lodge after a spending his second long day on the lake. "Where are Tom's things?"

"Everything's in his room," Fraser replied. He led George to the second-floor room and helped him pack up his brother's sketches, camping gear, and other personal items. It was all loaded onto the back of Fraser's wagon the next morning and taken to the Canoe Lake station, where George caught the train back to Owen Sound.

Two days later a strange object was spotted floating near an island less than a kilometre from Mowat Lodge. At first it appeared to be a dead loon, but when Larry Dickson and George

Rowe paddled over to investigate, they saw that most of it was submerged. They solemnly towed it to shore.

Everyone's worst fears were confirmed. "That's Tom — there's no mistake," someone said as soon as the body came out of the water. "It's Tom Thomson."

The news spread quickly — from Canoe Lake all the way down to Toronto, where the *Globe* wasted no time in following up its previous report with the story that confirmed everyone's worst fears:

TORONTO ARTIST DROWNS IN NORTH

The mystery surrounding the disappearance of Mr. Tom Thomson, the Toronto artist, at Canoe Lake, Algonquin Park, on Sunday, July 8, was solved yesterday by the finding of his body. Word which reached the city last night indicated that he had been drowned. His canoe was found adrift a few hours after Mr. Thomson was last seen, and the fate of the artist was a mystery until yesterday's gruesome discovery. His brother, Mr. George Thomson of New Haven, Conn., also a painter, who had been visiting the family home at Owen Sound last week when the news first came, went to the scene and joined for a time in the search. The body, it was stated in last night's telegram, will be buried in Algonquin Park, which had been the artist's happy sketching ground for years.

For the rest of his life, Thoreau MacDonald would always remember that terrible evening in the summer of 1917 when his father wearily made his way home to Thornhill after a day's work in Toronto. "He came out to where we were picking black currants in the same tangled garden that made such a stir in the Art World," he wrote. "He could barely speak as he told me that Tom had drowned up in the Park."

The discovery of Thomson's body at Canoe Lake ended any speculation that he might still be alive, but it proved to be just the beginning of a complex mystery that would never be solved. All that anyone knew for sure was that he was last seen alive by Shannon Fraser and a few others at Mowat Lodge, paddling off in the midday drizzle to catch a big trout in order to play a practical joke on Mark Robinson.

When Dickson and Rowe fished Thomson's decomposing body from the water, they noticed that the lower portion of one of his legs was firmly wrapped in fishing line. It also appeared that he had received a violent blow to the head.

The state of Thomson's body after several days in the lake meant that any medical examination would have been a stomach-turning experience. Much of the skin had come away from the flesh, and the overwhelming stench of decomposition would have given the attending doctor every reason to hurry up with his report and order the body buried as quickly as possible. This was exactly what happened. Thomson's body was wrapped in a canvas shroud and placed in a coffin, which was then sealed inside a larger pine box to reduce the chances of the terrible smell escaping.

The funeral was a rushed affair. Shannon Fraser's horse-drawn wagon bore the pine box up through the woods to the Canoe Lake cemetery — a tiny graveyard enclosed by a white picket fence. The box was lowered into the freshly dug ground while Martin Bletcher Sr. read a few passages from Robinson's Anglican hymn book. About a dozen of Thomson's Algonquin Park friends gathered around the grave to pay their last respects.

Winnie Trainor stood silently at the front of the group, her head bowed in grief. She could not speak. Whenever someone approached her to offer their condolences, she could only nod absently. She had lost her Tom.

"Short and simple, just as Tom would have wanted," Mark Robinson observed as the mourners made their way down the hill and headed back to Mowat Lodge to have a drink in their friend's honour.

Robinson was certainly right. It was too simple — in fact the whole story was about to take a macabre twist that no one could have predicted.

Thomson's body was buried at Canoe Lake before his family was even aware of its discovery in the water. Once the telegram was sent to Owen Sound, it was a matter of hours before Shannon Fraser received a telegram from an undertaker named Churchill in nearby Huntsville. It tersely informed him that the Thomson family had ordered him to retrieve Tom's body from the grave and have it shipped up to Leith. He would be arriving on the next train.

This was hardly surprising, as the family had not been consulted on the quick burial at Canoe Lake and was understandably upset with the arrangements. John and Margaret Thomson would certainly have wanted a proper burial for their son in the family plot next to his infant brother, James. And so, with Winnie Trainor acting as their intermediary in Hunstville, they sought out Mr. Churchill, undertaker in the largest town nearest

Canoe Lake, and sent him on this grim mission the day after Thomson's burial.

But according to Fraser's account of what happened next, Churchill's behaviour at Canoe Lake cast serious doubt on the possibility of Thomson's body being removed at all.

Describing the undertaker as a tall, dark man in a bowler hat and long black coat, Fraser recalled meeting Churchill at the Canoe Lake train station later that evening.

"Give me a hand with this, will you?" Churchill said, indicating the large metal casket sitting on a baggage cart. As they struggled to lift the heavy container onto the back of Fraser's wagon, Churchill explained that a case like this called for a metal casket, which could be tightly sealed and soldered shut so as to prevent the nauseating odour of the badly decomposed body escaping during the long train journey to Owen Sound.

"So you'll be doing your work tomorrow, I expect," Fraser said as he snapped the horses' reigns and they set off for Mowat Lodge.

"Tonight," Churchill replied. "I want to get out on the morning train and get this coffin off to Owen Sound tomorrow."

"But I doubt if I can find you any help at this time of night," Fraser replied, glancing at his pocket watch. It was now past eight o'clock and the sun was about to disappear behind the western hills.

"I don't need any help. Just get me a good digging shovel, a lantern, and a crowbar. I'll do the rest."

Fraser could not believe his ears. "You can't do all that without any help!"

"Yes I can. Just pick me up at midnight and we'll deliver this casket to the train station. I don't want to be here any longer than I have to."

Still shaking his head in disbelief, Fraser stopped at Mowat Lodge to pick up some tools for Churchill, and then they continued up through the woods to the small cemetery — a trip he and the horses had made just the day before.

"So midnight," Fraser said as he and the undertaker set down the empty casket next to Thomson's fresh grave.

"I'll be ready," Churchill replied.

Fraser could hear the shovel digging into the loose, sandy earth as he climbed aboard his wagon and drove off through the dark woods. By now the sun had gone and the forest was almost pitch black. He chuckled to himself, fully expecting to return in three hours to find Churchill half dead from exhaustion and Tom's body still buried.

But when he later drove the horses back up the hill and followed the distant glow of Churchill's lantern through the trees, he found the undertaker sitting smugly atop the sealed metal casket, casually smoking a cigar.

"All done?"

"All done," Churchill replied. "Now give me a hand with this so we can get out of here."

As he lifted his end of the casket, Fraser could not help but notice how the load felt peculiar. He had helped carry Tom's wooden box containing his casket the day before, and it did not feel quite like this. Somehow, the distribution of the weight did not seem right for a dead body. He was about to say something to Churchill, but realized it would only elicit another caustic remark, so he stayed quiet.

They loaded the metal casket back onto the baggage section of Fraser's wagon and rode in silence to the train station, where the casket was tagged for delivery to Owen Sound.

All the while, Fraser kept wondering how on earth one man

could have possibly dug up a grave, opened a pine box, opened a casket, removed a badly decomposed body with his bare hands, reinstalled it in the metal casket, soldered the whole thing shut, then filled in the grave — all with just a shovel and crowbar, and in less than three hours!

There was no lingering odour, and Churchill appeared oddly clean and rested. Something definitely did not make sense.

On July 19, George Thomson was at the Owen Sound train station when Tom's sealed metal casket arrived. Along with the local undertaker, he accompanied the casket to the Thomson home, where the family received friends and neighbours with solemn dignity. Most of the people who came to pay their respects did not know Tom Thomson the artist, but rather the happy, mischievous boy and native son who had gone off and made good in the big city.

The sealed coffin could not be opened without a great deal of work and mess, not to mention the overpowering stench of its contents. The grief-stricken Thomsons had no way of knowing for certain that it contained the body of their Tom. They simply had to rely on Churchill's word that it did.

The funeral was simple and tasteful. Surrounded by his parents, aunt, and siblings, not to mention dozens of family friends, Tom's casket was taken to Knox United Church in Owen Sound for the funeral service. Later, the long procession made its way through the town and then headed northeast a few kilometres to Leith, Tom's childhood home, where the casket was lowered into the ground in the family plot — within view of Rose Hill.

As far as the family was concerned, Tom Thomson was finally home.

* * *

Meanwhile, back in Algonquin Park, another drama was playing out among the locals. On the morning following the midnight exhumation of Thomson's body, Ranger Mark Robinson had dropped by the Canoe Lake station to meet the out-going train, just as he did every day, to check for fur poachers. The first person he encountered was the undertaker Churchill, who was preparing to have the metal casket loaded onto the train.

"What have you got there?" Robinson asked.

"And what's it to you?" was Churchill's reply.

Robinson identified himself as the local ranger, and Churchill bowed sheepishly. "This is the body of Mr. Thomas Thomson," he said. "It's being shipped to his family in Owen Sound."

"You can't do that," Robinson shot back. "That body was legally buried — you need official permission from the park …"

"No, I do not," said Churchill, shaking his head. "When I get instructions to remove a body, I do so."

Robinson immediately went into the station and telephoned his boss, the park superintendent. George Bartlett had always been fond of Thomson, but by now he was growing tired of all the commotion surrounding the drowning and feared it was drawing too much bad publicity for Algonquin Park.

"With all due respect to Tom, just let the undertaker take the body and be done with it, Mark," Bartlett said. "But make sure he filled in that grave up at the cemetery."

Robinson obeyed. He sadly watched his friend's casket loaded onto the baggage car, remembering how just two weeks earlier they had been fishing together for that big old trout near the Joe Lake Dam. Once the train was slowly making its way around the bend in a cloud of steam and smoke, Robinson headed straight down to Canoe Lake and the little burial ground in the woods.

What he found supported Shannon Fraser's claim that Thomson's body had not been removed after all. There was a shallow hole, roughly the area of a coffin, at Thomson's gravesite — as if a coffin had been removed. But there were no other signs on the ground to indicate that any heavy lifting or other work had taken place. And where were the original coffin and pine box? Had Churchill actually dug them both up and placed them inside the metal coffin? Impossible! They would never have fit inside the metal casket anyway. The more Robinson stared at the scene before him, the more it appeared that the undertaker had simply dug half a metre down, shovelled the earth into his metal casket, soldered it shut, and waited for Fraser to pick him up.

Then it occurred to him — and he hated the very thought of it — but maybe his friend Shan Fraser was in on the whole thing!

Thomson was not dead for more than a few weeks before the rumours began. Some believed that Winnie Trainor had another suitor who was determined to get rid of his rival, and had ambushed Thomson on the lake. Others believed that Martin Bletcher Jr. had killed Thomson over the flag-swapping incidents and their ongoing arguments over the family's pro-German sympathies.

Another theory was that Shannon Fraser had accidentally killed Thomson in a drunken fight over the money Thomson had lent him and now needed to be repaid so that he could buy a suit for his wedding to Winnie. In order to cover his tracks, Fraser was said to have bound Thomson's legs with fishing line and attached a weight to them, taken his body out on the lake and dumped it overboard, then set his overturned canoe adrift on the lake.

There was no shortage of fanciful theories, all supported by at least some shred of evidence. But Thomson's closest friends and sketching companions looked at the coroner's report and drew the simplest conclusion of all: he had simply stood up in his canoe to relive himself, lost his balance, hit his head on the side of the canoe as it overturned, and toppled into the water, unconscious. This was further supported by the well-known fact that he often kept a bottle of whisky secured under one of the thwarts of his canoe. The fishing line wrapped around his leg could have been there to support a twisted ankle — so a combination of the weak ankle and tipsiness could have made him lose his balance. This simple explanation was never given much attention, perhaps because it was just too simple.

For the next forty years, the mystery of Tom Thomson's death continued to puzzle anyone who discussed it. The residents of Canoe Lake grew old, and some went to their own graves still speculating over what had happened. Mowat Lodge burned down, more cottages and summer camps were built along the lake, and eventually the entire community had evolved into something completely different from what Thomson had known. But the mystery of his death remained a popular topic, not only in Algonquin Park but also further afield as Thomson's fame as an artist continued to grow through his bold, colourful images of the north country.

Was Thomson killed by a blow to the head in a drunken fight with Shannon Fraser over money, or in a fight with Martin Bletcher Jr. over the German's anti-Canadian sympathies during the war — or even by a jealous rival for the hand of Winnie Trainor? The circumstances surrounding Thomson's last days made it easy to concoct possible explanations, especially after many years had passed and the principal suspects had died.

Even the mystery of Thomson's final resting place was further complicated by hearsay that Shannon Fraser had always known the undertaker Churchill did not exhume Thomson's body that night, because there was no body to exhume. It was suggested that Fraser had panicked when he received Churchill's telegram informing him he would be on the next train from Huntsville. Fearing that Churchill might find incriminating evidence on Thomson's hastily buried corpse, Fraser could have rushed through the woods to dig up the body himself, then reburied it in a shallow grave a safe distance away before going to meet Churchill at the train station.

Logically, if Thomson's body was still in the Canoe Lake cemetery, either in its original spot or a few metres away, its discovery might finally prove or disprove the allegations of murder, or whether the undertaker had in fact done the seemingly impossible and single-handedly exhumed Thomson's decomposed body and shipped it home to Owen Sound.

The questions and theories continued to circulate around the Canoe Lake community until the autumn of 1956. That was when four local men — Bill Little, Gibby Gibson, Frank Braught, and Jack Eastaugh — decided to take things into their own hands and dig up Thomson's body — if they could find it. They knew it was illegal to exhume a body without permission, but Little was well-versed in the law and was confident that if they solved the mystery, any legal implications would automatically take care of themselves. In this special case, they believed the end justified the means.

Besides, there was a distinct possibility that no body would be found, which meant there was no crime to commit.

So one drizzly autumn day, the four friends set off into the woods to find the overgrown Canoe Lake cemetery and, hopefully, the grave of Tom Thomson. They eventually found a grave hidden beneath a spruce tree, which had apparently grown naturally over the gravesite since some point after 1917. Inside it, they found the bones of a man they were convinced was Tom Thomson.

But the four men's triumph was short-lived. Although the skull found in the Canoe Lake grave had a hole in the temple, supporting the medical report that Thomson had received a hard blow to the head, an official examination of the bones revealed they were not Thomson's. In fact, the evidence pointed to the bones being those of a Native man considerably shorter than Thomson. How this man's body ended up in the grave became a mystery in itself, as there were no official records of another burial at the site. Through the years, the Thomson family steadfastly refused to exhume the metal casket from the Leith

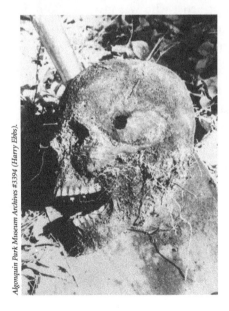

Algonquin Park Museum Archives #3394 (Harry Ebbs).

Tom Thomson's skull, exhumed from the Canoe Lake cemetery by William Little and his friends in 1956, was first believed to be that of another man. Recent forensic evidence has determined that it does in fact belong to Thomson.

cemetery, so at the time it could not be determined whether the artist's body ever made it home.

As time passed, the Tom Thomson mystery grew more baffling. From stories of a ghostly figure paddling on Canoe Lake to several books and documentary films devoted to the subject, the mystery became a part of Canadian culture. As we now approach the centennial of Thomson's death, there has still been no concrete evidence to support how he died. Whether it was an accident or murder — with arguments for manslaughter and suicide thrown into the mix — we will probably never know the truth. The trail has simply grown too cold.

But there has been a recent breakthrough in the question of Thomson's final resting place. In his 2010 book *Northern Light*, author and *Globe and Mail* columnist Roy MacGregor reported that the skull found in the Canoe Lake grave by Little, Gibson, Eastaugh, and Braught back in 1956 was in fact Thomson's. This was determined by a forensic artist who was given a photo of the skull — without being told who it was believed to be — and asked to draw a face to it. The face she produced was instantly recognizable as Thomson's.

Though not as convincing as DNA evidence, which cannot be obtained without the participation of Thomson's descendants, MacGregor's revelation supports the long-held theory that the undertaker Churchill did not bother to exhume Thomson and simply shipped a casket half-filled with earth to Owen Sound.

The hole in that skull, however, tells us that whichever way Thomson met his end, it was violent.

10

Establishing the Icon

Alex Jackson was severely wounded in the front-line trenches of Belgium in June 1916, and was sent to England to recover. More than a year later he was in a retraining camp at Shoreham, preparing to be shipped back to the war, when mail call brought a devastating letter from Toronto. That was when Jim MacDonald informed him of "an empty canoe and an artist missing in far-off Algonquin Park."

The news struck Jackson like another enemy bullet, and he dropped the letter in despair. More than anything else, the one thing that had kept him going through the past two years, through all the mud, blood, barbed wire, and artillery explosions, was the promise that once the war was over he would soon be back sketching with Thomson in Algonquin Park.

Now that could never be.

"I could sit down and cry to think that while in all this

turmoil over here the peace and quietness of the north country should be the scene of such a tragedy," Jackson wrote back to MacDonald. "Without Tom the north country seems a desolation of bush and rock. He was the guide, the interpreter, and we the guests partaking of his hospitality so generously given."

Arthur Lismer was also deeply shocked by the news. "We've lost a big man — both as an artist and a fine character," he wrote to Dr. MacCallum from Halifax, his heart heavy with grief. "When one recalls the few years that he had been painting, it is remarkable what he achieved. He has added a new note into all his associates, just as he made his art sing with a lively Canadian note. He was the simplest soul and the most direct worker I ever knew. Whilst we others speculated as to how it should be done, Tom did it with that amazing freshness that was always an inspiration to look at."

One of the hardest things MacDonald and Dr. MacCallum ever had to do was go into the shack behind the Studio Building for the first time after Thomson died. It had been locked up since late winter, and when they entered the dusty room they found the results of his last months at the big easel.

Seeing all of Thomson's work together for the first time was a moving experience. Resting on the easel, still awaiting completion, was *The West Wind*, painted from the sketch Thomson had been working on the day the big pine nearly fell on him, Dr. MacCallum recalled. The two men also found *The Pointers*, Thomson's red-dominated rebuttal to the hostile critics, and *The Drive*, another unfinished canvas depicting a jam of logs beneath the dam at Grand Lake.

There were several other canvases they had never seen before — not to mention dozens upon dozens of oil sketches on wooden panels, all stacked on the table, the shelves and hanging on the walls.

"Look at this," MacDonald said as he stood solemnly before *The Jack Pine*, leaning against the wall. Its bold, brick-like brushstrokes stood out in the bright sunlight shining through the shack window. The two marvelled at the subtle differences in colour from brushstroke to brushstroke in the sky and in the lake.

"It's amazing how far Tom progressed in just a few short years," MacDonald remarked.

Dr. MacCallum agreed. "He certainly was creating work that was truly new and original."

"One can only imagine what he would have achieved, had he lived …"

It was heartbreaking.

As September arrived and the first few maple and birch leaves started to change colour, Thomson's fellow artist and Studio Building neighbour Bill Beatty took the train up to Canoe Lake on a special mission. Though now in his late forties, he still had enough energy to complete a task that would have daunted many younger men. Several tons of large rocks had to be hauled up the hill at Hayhurst Point, just across the water from Mowat Lodge. This spot was chosen because it overlooked the small clearing where Thomson often set up his tent. Shannon Fraser rounded up a few local men to help Beatty find enough rocks and carry them up the hill — but it was still a long, exhausting task that must have taken at least a couple of days to complete.

Once he had enough rocks assembled, Beatty got busy with a trowel, carefully stacking and cementing them together to form a tall, sturdy cairn. Jim and Thoreau MacDonald arrived in Algonquin Park that weekend, bringing with them a bronze plaque to be installed onto the front of the cairn. MacDonald had called upon all his skills as a designer to create the lettering on the plaque, which all the Studio Building artists agreed was a touching and fitting tribute to their late friend:

TO THE MEMORY OF
TOM THOMSON
ARTIST, WOODSMAN AND GUIDE
WHO WAS DROWNED IN CANOE LAKE
JULY 8TH 1917
HE LIVED HUMBLY BUT PASSIONATELY WITH THE WILD
IT MADE HIM BROTHER TO ALL UNTAMED
THINGS OF NATURE
IT DREW HIM APART AND REVEALED ITSELF
WONDERFULLY TO HIM
IT SENT HIM OUT FROM THE WOOD ONLY TO SHOW
THESE REVELATIONS THROUGH HIS ART AND
IT TOOK HIM TO ITSELF AT LAST

Nearly a century later, the cairn remains in place overlooking Canoe Lake, standing strong against the elements — much like the weather-beaten old trees Thomson depicted in his best-known paintings, *The Jack Pine* and *The West Wind*.

As Thomson's closest friends, mentors, patrons, and unofficial agents, it was left up to MacDonald and Dr. MacCallum to sort through his artwork and to catalogue all the paintings for the artist's estate.

This would not be easy; in less than five years, Thomson had painted about three hundred sketches on wood panels and about twenty-five canvases. The sketches were scattered everywhere, and to make matters worse, most of them were unsigned. Working with the blessing of Thomson's brother George, MacDonald and Beatty solved much of the problem by designing a special dye stamp that could be applied to the back or a bottom corner of each sketch. This would not only substitute for the signature but also authenticate the work as a genuine Thomson. For weeks they searched for any sketches the artist may have sold or given away, and they were duly stamped with a logo that incorporated TT and 1917 inside the outline of a palette. Finally, as far as they knew, the only panels left unstamped were part of the series of sketches of the unfolding spring Thomson had completed shortly before his death. These were said to have been taken by George Thomson when he collected Tom's personal belongings and returned to the family home in Owen Sound.

Jackson was back in Toronto before the Armistice was signed. He had spent the last year of the war working as an artist on the staff of the Canadian War Memorials, and had been sent back to Canada to prepare for his next assignment — a trip to Siberia. Still in uniform, Jackson visited his friends at the Studio Building and was shown the collection of Thomson's life's work, all carefully sorted, authenticated, and neatly stored in a corner of one of the studios.

"We must have a big show of Tom's work," Jackson said when he saw just how much breath-taking material his friend had produced in such a short time. "The new Toronto Gallery would be the perfect space for a memorial retrospective."

Harris and MacDonald nodded. "We have been working on

just such an idea," MacDonald replied. "How would you like to write a brief essay for the catalogue?"

Jackson not only agreed, but he immediately got in touch with some Montreal friends to help arrange a show of Thomson's work in that city. "Tom's stuff will be a real eye-opener to them," he said of his hometown, which he believed to be hopelessly conservative when it came to accepting modern art. Thomson's colourful landscapes and daring compositions were sure to make Montreal critics wake up and take notice of what was going on in Toronto, he reasoned.

MacDonald and Dr. MacCallum agreed on a selection of canvases and they were shipped down to Montreal. *Exhibition of Paintings by the Late Tom Thomson* opened at Montreal's Arts Club, where it hung for three weeks before moving to the nearby Art Association of Montreal — now known as the Montreal Museum of Fine Arts.

The newspaper reviews were positive, but, much to Jackson's disappointment, the show did little to stir up any interest in what the Studio Building artists were trying to do.

The following year, Thomson was finally honoured in Toronto with a large retrospective show titled *Memorial Exhibition of Paintings by Tom Thomson*, which opened at the Art Gallery of Toronto in February 1920. Again, reviews were positive but not enthusiastic.

By the summer of 1919, two years after Thomson's death, many of his artist friends who had been scattered by the war were all back in Toronto. Jackson and Fred Varley had served overseas as war artists, sketching the devastated battlegrounds of France and Belgium; Frank Johnston and Arthur Lismer had stayed in Canada but painted images of the war effort on the home front. Meanwhile, Jim MacDonald and Frank Carmichael had struggled to continue their commercial art work in a much-diminished market.

Lawren Harris, who had served briefly as a musketry instructor at Camp Borden, Ontario, suffered a nervous breakdown and was ordered by his doctor to take a restful vacation. He did so in 1918, inviting Dr. MacCallum to join him on a train trip up north, past Sault Ste. Marie and along the eastern shore of Lake Superior. There, in the Algoma region, they found an opulent, unspoiled wilderness — a landscape painter's paradise. Harris wasted no time in organizing a return trip with MacDonald, Johnston, and Dr. MacCallum, and the later exhibition of their works from that trip was a great success.

Throughout it all, the quest to paint Canada in its own spirit remained firmly in the artists' minds, and now the time was right to make their statement. There seemed to be a renewed sense of national pride across Canada following the war. It was as if Canada had now come of age as a nation, having recently participated in a global event on an equal footing with other countries, suffering its own devastating losses on the battlefields and scoring its own rousing victories — from the Battles of Ypres to Vimy Ridge. Moreover, the war had also softened the attitudes of some critics, who now seemed much more accepting of modern art.

With all these conditions now in their favour — and the spirit of Tom Thomson's work inspiring them — five of his artist friends were invited to Harris's house one night in March 1920 to discuss plans for a large exhibition of their recent work. Although Jackson was away sketching at Georgian Bay at the time, he was included in the group. There would be seven of them in all — Carmichael, Harris, Jackson, Johnston, Lismer,

Tom Thomson's closest artist friends — the Group of Seven — are seen here in Toronto's Arts and Letters Club three years after Thomson's death. Frank Carmichael is the only member absent from this 1920 photo, which shows (clockwise around the table from bottom left) A.Y. Jackson, Fred Varley, Lawren Harris, non-member Professor Barker Fairley, Frank Johnston, Arthur Lismer, and J.E.H. MacDonald.

MacDonald, and Varley — so they simply titled their exhibition Group of Seven, and the name stuck.

Had Thomson lived, he certainly would have been included, bringing the total number to eight.

The Group of Seven exhibition opened at the Art Gallery of Toronto on May 7, 1920, not long after Thomson's memorial show. The artists had been bracing themselves for the worst, but were pleasantly surprised when all the newspaper reviews were either kind or downright enthusiastic.

Although none of Thomson's paintings were included in this show, the Group of Seven's success drew attention to their late friend, and demand for Thomson's works grew. Within just a few years his name was as well known as the Group of Seven.

This was largely thanks to Dr. MacCallum, who not only promoted Thomson's work every chance he got, but also worked closely with the artist's family when it came to selling the sketches and canvases. Several works sold easily. In 1918, the National Gallery's budget was severely depleted due to the war, but it nevertheless came up with seven hundred and fifty dollars to buy *The Jack Pine* for its ever-growing Thomson collection. But to the utter bewilderment of Dr. MacCallum and the Group of Seven, *The Jack Pine*'s counterpart, *The West Wind*, failed to find a buyer. For the next eight years it remained stored in the Studio Building, despite the urgings of Jackson and Harris that it should be on permanent exhibit in a major art gallery.

Finally, determined that the Art Gallery of Toronto should buy *The West Wind*, Dr. MacCallum approached the gallery's directors and offered it for sale for $1,500, believing they could not pass it up — but the offer was politely refused.

"This is an outrage!" Jackson gruffly replied when he heard the news. "Tom deserves to be represented by a major canvas in the Toronto gallery!"

Many others agreed with Jackson, and it wasn't long before members of the Canadian Club of Toronto rallied to the cause. In 1926 they raised the $1,500 and bought *The West Wind* from the artist's estate, through Dr. MacCallum, and immediately presented it as a gift to the Art Gallery of Toronto.

Today, *The West Wind* is widely considered to be Thomson's finest work, having edged past *The Jack Pine* for that honour, and it remains on exhibit in the same Toronto gallery, now known as the Art Gallery of Ontario.

* * *

When Dr. MacCallum died in 1943, his entire collection of paintings was bequeathed to the National Gallery. It was a major acquisition for the Gallery, with no less than one hundred and thirty-four works going into the public collection. Of these, the vast majority were works by Thomson which Dr. MacCallum had acquired from the artist over their six-year friendship.

A year later, in 1944, Thomson was introduced to a new generation of Canadians when the National Film Board of Canada produced a colour documentary on his life and work. Titled *West Wind* after what was by now his most famous canvas, the twenty-two-minute film traced Thomson's brief painting career through still images and footage of Algonquin Park. The producers invited Jackson, Harris, and Lismer to appear onscreen to comment on their late friend's influence upon the Group of Seven and modern Canadian art. The film also included footage of an elderly and feeble Dr. MacCallum showing off some of the many Thomson sketches in his vast collection.

Meanwhile, the Studio Building would remain virtually unchanged, standing on quiet Severn Street as a home to artists and a centre for creative thought in Toronto. Harris sold the property in 1948, but Jackson stayed on as a tenant until 1955. Thomson's shack, which by now had become the stuff of legend among Canadian artists, remained standing in the rear, and was occupied by a variety of tenants over the years. One of them, a prospector named Keith MacIver, was a good friend of Jackson. Throughout the 1930s, Jackson's winter morning ritual included joining MacIver for breakfast in the shack before returning to his studio for the day's work. Over the years, Arthur Lismer, Fred Varley, and several other artists worked in the shack, but even though Thomson only occupied it for two winters, the romantic notion of the woodsman living near the corner of Yonge and Bloor streets as if he were deep in the northern bush captured the imaginations of many Canadians.

As the legend of Tom Thomson continued to grow throughout Canada, so did the legend of his humble shack in the middle of the big city. In 1962, Robert and Signe McMichael negotiated with Studio Building owner Gordon MacNamara to buy the shack. Always fiercely protective of the Studio Building and its cultural significance, MacNamara was reluctant at first, but he finally agreed to the sale. Plank by plank, the shack was carefully dismantled and moved to the grounds of the McMichael Canadian Art Collection in nearby Kleinburg, where it remains a popular attraction as a small museum devoted to Thomson's life and times.

Throughout the 1960s, fifty years after Thomson's most productive seasons in Algonquin Park, his status in Canadian art circles showed no sign of letting up. In 1967 — Canada's centennial year — Canada Post honoured Thomson by reproducing *The Jack Pine* on its ten-cent postage stamp. That same year the Tom Thomson Art Gallery opened its doors in Owen Sound. It was not only named in honour of the hometown hero but also housed a significant collection of his work.

Then, in what was the largest Group of Seven event to date, the fiftieth anniversary of their inaugural exhibition was celebrated by a major show organized by the National Gallery of Canada. Curated by prominent Canadian art historian Dennis Reid, the exhibition placed Thomson firmly within the ranks of his seven friends by including his most famous canvases and many of his most important sketches — even though none of his work had been exhibited in the original Group of Seven show back in 1920.

The following year Thomson was front and centre across Canada once again when the major retrospective exhibition *The Art of Tom Thomson* opened at the Art Gallery of Ontario. It later travelled to Regina, Winnipeg, Montreal, and Charlottetown.

Most recently, Thomson's memory was honoured in the town of Hunstville, where he often stopped on his way to and from Algonquin Park to spend a few days at the home of Winnie Trainor. In 2005, sculptor Brenda Wainman-Goulet completed a life-size bronze of Thomson seated with his canoe, his sketchbox on his lap and his pipe hanging from his mouth as he concentrates on his colourful sketch of *The West Wind*. The bronze now graces the town square in downtown Hunstville.

Nearly a century has now passed since Tom Thomson paddled his canoe along the lakes and rivers of Algonquin Park, following the changing seasons as he searched for the colours and rhythms in nature that he could use to express himself in paint on a small birch panel — and perhaps later on a large canvas. His direct approach to painting, as well as his skills as a woodsman, were an inspiration to seven of his friends who went on to establish a vibrant form of modern landscape art that Canada could call its own. All these years later, the Group of Seven remains Canada's most enduring and influential art movement — and Tom Thomson's groundbreaking work forms a major part of their legacy.

Thomson's feats and skills as a woodsman have definitely been exaggerated through the retelling of his life over the decades. He was indeed good with a canoe, as well as an experienced camper and fisherman, but he was far from the idealized man of the wilderness that his city-bred friends would later describe. And even though he painted technically daring images such as *The Jack Pine*, he did not live long enough to fully develop confidence in his own abilities as an artist.

One thing that can never be exaggerated is Thomson's influence on his contemporaries and later generations of Canadian artists.

As A.Y. Jackson wrote shortly after his friend's mysterious, untimely death, "Well it is a blessing that the last years of his life were devoted as they were. He has blazed a trail where others may follow, and we will never go back to the old days again."

Chronology of Tom Thomson (1877–1917)

Thomson and His Times	Canada and the World
1806 Thomas "Tam" Thomson (grandfather) is born in Aberdeenshire, Scotland.	
	1832 Edouard Manet, future Impressionist painter, is born in France on January 23.
1833 Tam Thomson arrives in Upper Canada and buys land in Pickering Township, east of Toronto. Elizabeth Brodie (grandmother) arrives in Upper Canada with her family from Peterhead, Aberdeenshire.	
	1837 In France, Louis Daguerre invents the first practical photographic process, paving the way for modern photography.

Thomson and His Times	*Canada and the World*
	In England, Queen Victoria ascends the throne.
1839 Tam Thomson marries Elizabeth Brodie in Claremont, Ontario.	
1840 Father, John Thomson, is born in Claremont, Ontario.	**1840** Claude Monet, future Impressionist painter, is born in France on November 14.
1842 Mother, Margaret Matheson, is born in Ross, Prince Edward Island.	
	1854 The Crimean War pits Britain, France, and Turkey against Russia.
	1855 William Brymner, future artist and teacher, is born in Scotland on December 14.
1859 John Thomson and Margaret Matheson are married in Claremont, Ontario. They move into a new house built for them on the Thomson family farm.	**1859** In Quebec, the Victoria Bridge is completed, connecting the island of Montreal to the mainland and bringing more business to the city.
	1860 The Prince of Wales (later Edward VII) officially opens the Victoria Bridge.

Thomson and His Times

Canada and the World

Civil War breaks out in the United States, pitting the northern Union states against the southern Confederacy.

1865
The American Civil War ends; President Abraham Lincoln is assassinated on April 14.

James Wilson Morrice, future Canadian artist, is born in Montreal on August 10.

Robert Henri, future American artist, is born on June 25.

1866
Maurice Cullen, future Canadian artist, is born in Newfoundland on June 6.

1867
Canada is formed on July 1, as the British North America Act unites Ontario, Quebec, Nova Scotia, and New Brunswick.

1868
George Thomson (brother) is born in Claremont, Ontario.

1869
Elizabeth Thomson (sister) is born in Claremont, Ontario.

1869
Henri Matisse, future French artist, is born in France on December 31.

Thomson and His Times	**Canada and the World**
	1870 Under Emperor Napoleon III, France goes to war against Prussia.
	Manitoba joins Confederation.
1871 Henry Thomson (brother) is born in Claremont, Ontario.	**1871** British Columbia joins Confederation.
	The Franco-Prussian war ends. France's defeat ends the Second Empire, which is replaced by the Third Republic.
	Emily Carr, future Canadian artist, is born in Victoria, British Columbia, on December 13.
1873 Louise Thomson (sister) is born in Claremont, Ontario.	**1873** Claude Monet paints the radical *Impression: Sunrise* in Le Havre, France. The title will lend its name to a revolutionary art movement.
	Prince Edward Island joins Confederation.
	J.E.H. MacDonald is born in England on May 12.
1874 Elizabeth Brodie Thomson (sister) dies in Claremont, Ontario.	

Thomson and His Times	*Canada and the World*
1875 Thomas "Tam" Thomson dies in Claremont, Ontario.	
Minnie Thomson (sister) is born in Claremont, Ontario.	
1877 August 5: Thomas John Thomson is born on the family farm in Claremont, Ontario.	
Autumn: The Thomson family moves north to Rose Hill, a farm in Leith, Ontario, on Georgian Bay.	
1880 Ralph Thomson (brother) is born in Leith, Ontario.	**1880** The Royal Canadian Academy of Arts and the National Gallery of Canada are created by Canada's Governor General, the Marquis of Lorne.
	1881 Pablo Picasso, future artist, is born in Spain on October 25.
	Clarence Gagnon, future Canadian artist, is born in Montreal on November 8.
	Frederick Varley is born in Sheffield, England on January 2.
1882 James Brodie Thomson (brother) is born in Leith, Ontario.	**1882** Alex Young (A.Y.) Jackson is born in Montreal on October 3.

Thomson and His Times	Canada and the World
	David Milne is born in Ontario on January 8.
	James Wilson Morrice enters University College, Toronto.
1883 James Brodie Thomson (brother) dies in infancy in Leith, Ontario.	
1884 Margaret Thomson (sister) is born in Leith, Ontario.	**1884** Métis leader Louis Riel moves to the Saskatchewan Valley to help his people obtain their legal rights.
	1885 The Northwest Rebellion is put down. Its leader, Louis Riel, is hanged in Regina.
	Lawren Harris is born in Brantford, Ontario, on October 23.
	Arthur Lismer is born in England on June 27.
	The Canadian Pacific Railway is completed, linking Canada from coast to coast by rail and telegraph.
1886 Fraser Thomson (brother) is born in Leith, Ontario	**1886** The City of Vancouver is officially incorporated.

Thomson and His Times

Canada and the World

1887
The British Empire celebrates
Queen Victoria's Golden Jubilee.

1889
In Paris, the Eiffel Tower is
completed on the Champ de
Mars, next to the River Seine.

1890
Dutch painter Vincent van Gogh
commits suicide in France on
July 29.

Franklin Carmichael is born in
Ontario on October 24.

1891
Painter Georges Seurat dies in
France on March 29.

Canada's first prime minister, Sir
John A. Macdonald, dies in office
in Ottawa on June 6.

1895
In France, brothers Louis and
Auguste Lumière invent the
cinematograph and begin
making the first motion pictures.

1896
In Canada, Liberal Wilfrid
Laurier becomes the country's
first French-Canadian prime
minister.

Thomson and His Times	*Canada and the World*
	1897 Gold is discovered along the Klondike River, sparking a fervent gold rush that will draw thousands of prospectors to the Yukon over the next few years. William Brymner introduces James Wilson Morrice to Maurice Cullen in Ste. Anne de Beaupré, Quebec, where they paint winter landscapes.
1898 On his twenty-first birthday, Thomson comes into an inheritance of approximately $2,000 from the estate of his grandfather.	**1898** In Canada, the temperance movement gains nation-wide popularity, but the government says there is not enough support to pass a law prohibiting the sale of alcohol.
1899 Thomson attempts to enlist as a soldier in the Boer War, but is refused on medical grounds. Thomson is employed by the Kennedy & Sons foundry in Owen Sound as an apprentice machinist.	**1899** Canada sends troops to South Africa to fight for England in the Boer War.
1900 Thomson moves to Chatham, Ontario, where he attends the Canadian Business College.	**1900** Paris hosts a huge world's fair that attracts an estimated fifty million visitors.

Thomson and His Times

1901
Thomson moves to Seattle, Washington, to attend the Acme Business College.

He is employed as an elevator boy at the Diller Hotel.

1902
Thomson is employed by Maring & Ladd (later Maring & Blake), an engraving company in Seattle.

1904
Thomson works at the Seattle Engraving Company.

Thomson begins courting local girl Alice Lambert.

Canada and the World

1901
In London, Queen Victoria dies after sixty-four years on the British throne on January 22. She is succeeded by her son, Edward VII.

1902
French sculptor Auguste Rodin completes his masterpiece, *The Thinker*.

1903
French painter Paul Gauguin dies in Tahiti on May 8.

The age of aviation is born when American inventors Orville and Wilbur Wright demonstrate the first mechanized aircraft in Kitty Hawk, North Carolina.

Henry Ford establishes the Ford Motor Company in Dearborn, Michigan.

1904
Work begins on the Panama Canal.

Thomson and His Times

1905

After Alice Lambert refuses his marriage proposal, Thomson returns to Owen Sound.

Thomson moves to Toronto and joins the art department of Legg Brothers, commercial designers.

1906

Thomson enrolls in night classes at the Central Ontario School of Art and Design, where he studies briefly under artist William Cruickshank.

1908

Thomson is hired by Albert Robson to work in the art department of Grip Limited, under senior designer J.E.H. MacDonald.

John and Margaret Thomson sell Rose Hill and move to Owen Sound.

Canada and the World

1905

Paul-Emile Borduas, future Canadian painter, is born in Sainte Hilaire, Quebec, on November 1.

Alberta and Saskatchewan join Confederation.

1906

Post-Impressionist painter Paul Cézanne dies in France on October 22.

1907

Pablo Picasso paints *Demoiselles d'Avignon* in Paris.

A.Y. Jackson arrives in Paris to study at the Académie Julian.

1908

The Arts and Letters Club is founded in Toronto.

In Ottawa, Sir Wilfrid Laurier is elected prime minister for the fourth and last time.

1910

A.Y. Jackson paints *The Edge of the Maple Wood* in Sweetsburg, Quebec.

Thomson and His Times

Canada and the World

In England, King Edward VII dies on May 6. He is succeeded by his son, George V.

1911
Thomson meets Arthur Lismer and Franklin Carmichael at Grip Limited.

1911
In Canada, the Conservatives under Robert Borden defeat Laurier's Liberals.

Thomson sketches at Lake Scugog with fellow Grip employee Ben Jackson.

A.Y. Jackson returns to Europe to paint in France and Italy.

At the Arts and Letters Club, Thomson meets Lawren Harris and Dr. James MacCallum.

1912
Spring: Thomson makes his first trip to Algonquin Park with Ben Jackson. There he meets Shannon Fraser and rangers Mark Robinson and Bud Callighen.

1912
The Art Association of Montreal opens a new gallery on Sherbrooke Street (now the Montreal Museum of Fine Arts).

Summer: Thomson takes an extended canoe trip through the Mississagi Forest Reserve with fellow Grip employee William Broadhead.

On its maiden voyage, the colossal *S.S. Titanic* strikes an iceberg and sinks in the North Atlantic near Newfoundland.

Fred Varley starts working at Grip Limited.

Thomson follows Albert Robson and several other employees from Grip Limited to Rous and Mann Press.

Thomson and His Times

1913

Winter: Thomson paints *A Northern Lake* on weekends at the Rous and Mann office.

April: He exhibits *A Northern Lake* at the Ontario Society of Artists' spring exhibition. It is bought by the Government of Ontario for $250.

Spring: Thomson returns to Algonquin Park, sketching and working as a guide. He stays through late autumn.

November: Thomson meets A.Y. Jackson at Lawren Harris's studio in Toronto.

Thomson accepts Dr. MacCallum's offer of one year of financial support if he devotes himself to painting.

1914

January: Thomson moves into the newly constructed Studio Building in Toronto, sharing a space with A.Y. Jackson. The building will eventually house Harris, MacDonald, Arthur Heming, Curtis Williamson, and Bill Beatty.

Moonlight is painted under Jackson's guidance.

Canada and the World

1913

A.Y. Jackson returns to Canada and in May visits Toronto, where he meets J.E.H. MacDonald, Arthur Lismer, and later Lawren Harris.

The Armory Show, a groundbreaking exhibition of modern art, is held in New York City.

More than 400,000 people immigrate to Canada, the largest number to arrive in one year.

A.Y. Jackson paints *Terre Sauvage.*

1914

Spring-summer: A.Y. Jackson and Bill Beatty paint in the Rocky Mountains while staying at construction camps of the Canadian Northern Railway.

In Hollywood, English comedian Charles Chaplin makes his first silent films at Keystone studios.

Thomson and His Times

He becomes a member of the Ontario Society of Artists.

Moonlight and *Morning Cloud* are exhibited at the Ontario Society of Artists' spring exhibition. *Moonlight* is bought by the National Gallery of Canada for $150.

May: Thomson returns to Algonquin Park with Arthur Lismer.

Spring-summer: Thomson travels by canoe from Algonquin Park to Parry Sound, then spends a few weeks at Dr. MacCallum's cottage on Georgian Bay. He returns to Algonquin Park by canoe.

Fall: Thomson sketches with A.Y. Jackson in Algonquin Park. They are later joined by Arthur Lismer and Fred Varley.

November: He returns to Toronto and attempts a second time to enlist in the army, but is turned away on medical grounds.

After Jackson's departure, Thomson now shares Studio Building space with Frank Carmichael.

Canada and the World

August: The First World War breaks when Great Britain and its allies declare war on Germany and Austria-Hungary. Canada immediately begins recruiting troops to be sent overseas.

Thomson and His Times

1915
Northern River is painted.

Northern River and *Split Rock, Georgian Bay* are exhibited in the Ontario Society of Artists' spring exhibition. *Northern River* is acquired by the National Gallery of Canada for $500.

Spring: Thomson returns to Algonquin Park, where he works as a guide and fire ranger.

Summer: Thomson visits Dr. MacCallum's cottage on Georgian Bay to measure walls for a series of decorative murals.

Late autumn: Thomson moves into the recently renovated shack behind the Studio Building. It will be his winter quarters for the next two years.

December: A one-man show of oil sketches is exhibited at the Arts and Letters Club.

Winter: *In the Northland* is painted.

1916
Spring Ice is exhibited in the Ontario Society of Artists' spring exhibition. It is purchased by the National Gallery of Canada for $300.

Canada and the World

1915
In Belgium, Canadian Forces withstand German poison gas attacks at the Battle of Ypres.

A.Y. Jackson enlists in the 60th Infantry Battalion (Victoria Rifles) and is sent overseas as part of the Third Canadian Division.

1916
In Canada, federal Opposition leader Laurier encourages young Quebecers to enlist, despite widespread opposition to the war in that province.

Thomson and His Times

Spring: Thomson returns to Algonquin Park, where he is visited by Lawren Harris and Dr. MacCallum.

Thomson works as a fire ranger in the park.

August: Travels by canoe to Petawawa Gorges.

Autumn: Thomson returns to his shack in Toronto and begins work on the canvases *The Pointers*, *The Drive*, *The West Wind*, and *The Jack Pine*.

1917
Early spring: Thomson arrives in Algonquin Park with the intention of documenting the changing season in a series of daily sketches.

May: Dr. MacCallum and his son, Arthur, visit Thomson in Algonquin Park.

July 7: Thomson paddles off for an afternoon of fishing. His overturned canoe is later found adrift on Canoe Lake.

July 8–16: Friends undertake a thorough search of the Canoe Lake area. Thomson's brother, George Thomson, arrives in Algonquin Park to assist with the search.

Canada and the World

J.E.H. MacDonald's *Tangled Garden* is exhibited at the Ontario Society of Artists' spring show. It touches off a storm of controversy in the Toronto press.

1917
In London, Lord Beaverbrook establishes the Canadian War Memorials program, which enlists Canadian artists to paint images of the war effort.

Despite suffering heavy casualties, Canadian soldiers score a major victory at the Battle of Vimy Ridge.

In December, Halifax is partially destroyed and thousands of people are killed or injured by a massive explosion when the French ship *Mont Blanc* collides with another vessel, setting off its cargo of explosives.

Thomson and His Times

July 16: Thomson's body is found floating on Canoe Lake. After a brief examination, it is buried at Canoe Lake Cemetery.

July 21: The Thomson family orders Mr. Churchill, an undertaker, to exhume the body and ship it home to Owen Sound for burial in the family plot. There is plenty of speculation at the time as to whether or not this was done.

September: Bill Beatty and J.E.H. MacDonald erect a cairn to Thomson's memory at Canoe Lake.

Autumn: The Arts and Letters Club holds a memorial exhibition of Thomson's work.

1918

J.E.H. MacDonald designs an identifying stamp for Thomson's unsigned sketches. He takes a careful inventory of Thomson's work and stores hundreds of paintings in the Studio Building.

The National Gallery of Canada purchases *The Jack Pine* from the Thomson estate.

Canada and the World

1918

The First World War ends on November 11; over eight million have died and twenty-one million have been wounded. Canadian deaths number sixty thousand.

The Canada Elections Act gives the vote to all women (except status Indians) in federal elections.

Thomson and His Times

1919
March: *Exhibition of Paintings by the Late Tom Thomson* held at the Arts Club, Montreal. It later moves to the Art Association of Montreal gallery.

1920
February: Tom Thomson Memorial Exhibition held at the Art Gallery of Toronto.

May: The Group of Seven holds its debut exhibition at the Art Gallery of Toronto.

Canada and the World

1919
The United States outlaws the sale of alcohol.

The Treaty of Versailles is signed in Paris, imposing harsh post-war penalties on Germany, which leads to much resentment.

Impressionist painter Pierre-Auguste Renoir dies in France on December 3.

Former Canadian prime minister Sir Wilfrid Laurier dies in Ottawa on February 17.

1920
Canada joins the League of Nations.

The Beaver Hall Group of modern artists is formed in Montreal. Several of its members are former students of William Brymner.

1921
W.L. Mackenzie King begins the first of three separate terms as prime minister of Canada. Agnes Macphail is the first woman elected to the Canadian Parliament.

1924
Canadian artist James Wilson Morrice dies in a military hospital in Tunis on January 23.

Thomson and His Times

Canada and the World

The controversial British Empire Exhibition at Wembley, England, attracts unprecedented attention for Canadian artists.

1925
Thomson's mother, Margaret Thomson, dies in Owen Sound.

1926
At age 86, father, John Thomson, marries his sister-in-law, Henrietta Matheson, age 80.

The Canadian Club purchases *The West Wind* from the Thomson estate for $1,500 and presents it to the Art Gallery of Toronto.

1926
Claude Monet dies in France on December 5.

1930
Thomson's father, John Thomson, dies in Owen Sound.

1943
The National Film Board of Canada produces *West Wind*, a documentary on the life and work of Tom Thomson.

1943
Dr. James MacCallum dies in Toronto on August 6.

1956
Eager to solve the longstanding mystery surrounding Thomson's final resting place, four friends — Bill Little, Gibby Gibson, Frank Braught, and Jack Eastaugh — exhume a body from the Canoe Lake gravesite. At the time, the

Thomson and His Times

Canada and the World

popular opinion is that it's not
Thomson's.

1962
Thomson's shack is removed
from its spot behind the Studio
Building and reassembled on
the grounds of the McMichael
Canadian at Collection at
Kleinburg, Ontario.

1969
Arthur Lismer dies in Montreal
on March 23.

Fred Varley dies in Toronto on
September 8.

1970
The fiftieth anniversary of the
Group of Seven's first exhibition
is celebrated by an exhibition
organized by the National
Gallery of Canada. Thomson's
work is prominently featured.

1970
Lawren Harris dies in Vancouver
on January 29.

2010
The remains found by Bill Little,
Gibby Gibson, Frank Braught,
and Jack Eastaugh at the Canoe
Lake gravesite are identified
by forensic experts as Tom
Thomson's.

Bibliography

Addison, Ottelyn and Elizabeth Harwood. *Tom Thomson: The Algonquin Years*. Toronto: McGraw-Hill Ryerson, 1969.

Davies, Blodwen. *Tom Thomson: The Story of a Man Who Looked for Beauty and Truth in the Wilderness*. Vancouver: Mitchell Press Ltd., 1967.

Hill, Charles C. *The Group of Seven: Art for a Nation*. Ottawa: National Gallery of Canada, 1995.

Housser, F.B. *A Canadian Art Movement: The Story of the Group of Seven*. Toronto: MacMillan, 1926.

Jackson, A.Y. *A Painter's Country*. Toronto: Clarke, Irwin & Co., 1958.

Larsen, Wayne. *A.Y. Jackson: The Life of a Landscape Painter*. Toronto: Dundurn Press, 2009.

Little, William T. *The Tom Thomson Mystery*. Toronto: McGraw-Hill, 1970.

MacDonald, Thoreau. *The Group of Seven*. Toronto: Ryerson Press, 1944.

MacGregor, Roy. *Northern Light: The Enduring Mystery of Tom Thomson and the Woman Who Loved Him*. Toronto: Random House, 2010.

McMichael, Robert. *One Man's Obsession*. Scarborough, ON: Prentice-Hall Canada, 1986.

Mellen, Peter. *The Group of Seven*. Toronto: McClelland and Stewart, 1970.

Murray, Joan. *The Best of Tom Thomson*. Edmonton: Hurtig, 1986.

_____. *Tom Thomson: Design for a Canadian Hero*. Toronto: Dundurn Press, 1998.

_____. *Tom Thomson: The Last Spring*. Toronto: Dundurn Press, 1994.

_____. *Tom Thomson: Trees*. Toronto: McArthur & Co., 1999.

Reid, Dennis. *The Group of Seven*. Ottawa: The National Gallery of Canada, 1970.

_____. *The MacCallum Bequest*. Ottawa: The National Gallery of Canada, 1969.

_____. and Charles C. Hill, *Tom Thomson*. Toronto: Art Gallery of Ontario/National Gallery of Canada/Douglas & McIntyre, 2002.

_____. *Tom Thomson: The Jack Pine*. Ottawa: The National Gallery of Canada, 1975.

Robson, Albert H. *Canadian Landscape Painters*. Toronto: Ryerson Press, 1932.

_____. *Tom Thomson*, Toronto: Ryerson Press, 1932.

Silcox, David P. *Tom Thomson: An Introduction to His Life and Art*. Toronto: Firefly, 2002.

Town, Harold and David P. Silcox. *Tom Thomson: The Silence and the Storm*. Toronto: McClelland and Stewart, 1977.

Index

Lismer, Esther, 94
Lismer, Marjorie, 94
Little, William, 17–24, 144–46, 178, 179
Little Cauchon Lake, Algonquin Park, 116

MacCallum, Doctor James, 62–63, 74–75, 77–82, 86, 87–88, 89–90, 92, 93–96, 99, 100, 103–08, 114–15, 116–18, 123–26, 128, 148–49, 150, 152, 153, 155, 156, 171, 172, 173, 174, 175, 178
MacDonald, J.E.H. (Jim), 57–59, 61–63, 66, 67–70, 74, 75–76, 78, 79–80, 87, 89, 97, 102, 105, 108, 110, 114–15, 120, 123–24, 136, 147–52, 153–54, 164, 170, 172, 175, 176
MacDonald, Joan, 58,
MacDonald, Thoreau, 58, 105, 108, 136, 150
Macdonald, Sir John A., 12, 167
MacGregor, Roy, 12, 146
MacNamara, Gordon, 157
Maring, C.C., 46, 49, 50–52
Matheson, Henrietta, 32, 178
McLean, Tom, 58, 59, 63, 64
McMichael, Robert, 157
McMichael, Signe, 157

McMichael Canadian Collection, Kleinburg, Ontario, 107, 157, 179
Mississagi River, 63, 171
Montreal, Quebec, 26, 75, 76, 97, 102, 152, 158, 162, 163, 165, 171, 177, 179
Moonlight, Early Evening (Thomson), 85
Mowat Lodge, 60, 84, 90, 94, 96, 110, 113, 122, 127, 129–32, 134, 136–37, 138–39, 143, 149

The National Gallery of Canada, 85, 102, 113, 155, 156, 157, 165, 173, 174, 176, 179
A Northern Lake (Thomson), 68, 69–70, 172
Northern Light, 12, 146
Northern River (Thomson), 13, 101–02, 110, 125, 174

Ontario Society of Artists, 68–69, 76, 85, 97, 101, 113, 114, 172, 173, 174, 175
Orillia, Ontario, 100
Ottawa River, 59, 119, 121
Owen Sound, Ontario, 13, 21, 33, 41–45, 46, 47, 53, 71,